MAKE NO SMALL PLANS

MAKE NO SMALL PLANS

Lessons on Thinking Big, Chasing Dreams, and Building Community

**Elliott Bisnow, Brett Leve,
Jeff Rosenthal, Jeremy Schwartz**

CURRENCY
NEW YORK

Published in the United States by Currency, an imprint of Random
House, a division of Penguin Random House LLC, New York.

CURRENCY and its colophon are trademarks of
Penguin Random House LLC.

Hardback ISBN 978-1-9848-2264-2
Ebook ISBN 978-1-9848-2265-9

PRINTED IN CANADA ON ACID-FREE PAPER

crownpublishing.com

2 4 6 8 9 7 5 3 1

FIRST EDITION

This book is dedicated to the entire Summit community.
For teaching us. For believing in us. For trusting us.

THE WORLD DOESN'T CHANGE ONE PERSON AT
A TIME. IT CHANGES AS NETWORKS OF
RELATIONSHIPS FORM AMONG PEOPLE WHO
DISCOVER THEY SHARE A COMMON CAUSE AND
VISION OF WHAT'S POSSIBLE. THIS IS GOOD NEWS
FOR THOSE OF US INTENT ON CHANGING THE WORLD
AND CREATING A POSITIVE FUTURE.

—MARGARET WHEATLEY

FOREWORD

When Elliott, Jeff, Brett, and Jeremy asked me to support Summit, which quickly and naturally turned into a CEO and partnership commitment, I first asked them what their underlying mission had been for the last decade. As a long-standing Summit community member and a multi-hyphenate company founder, maker, and artist, I'd long valued Summit for the camaraderie and community I found at their events—but I was never clear on what they were trying to achieve behind it all.

"Make No Small Plans," they said.

"But *why*?" I asked, beginning to apply design thinking to a thirteen-year-old early-stage start-up.

"Because life is precious, and it should be dedicated to doing something meaningful."

And that, I realized, is what the members of the Summit community have in common: the insatiable desire to create and connect so that we can make an impact on ourselves and on generations to come. Because those are the type of people we are. We work hard and play harder. We want to know that our spirit can ripple long after we're gone. And we often feel like outsiders, looking for others who work as hard, who care as much, and who take big ideas and turn them into real things in the world.

This book is the story of four friends with a bold vision, who held a belief that was being defined as it was being brought to life. It still is to this day. It will be for decades to come. Such is life for the ever-evolving entrepreneur.

Along the way, Elliott, Jeff, Brett, and Jeremy share their adventures, their mistakes, their discovery of their passion and purpose. The process of getting here was full of humility and heartbreak, success and failure, and all of the life lessons that fill the spaces between. Summit's story to date is also one of true "maker mind" and the ways human creativity can express itself through the artistic medium of business—my favorite medium of all.

I invite you to enjoy this ride, but more than anything, to see how innately human this story is. I hope you are inspired by the courage it took to get weird, the trust it took to take every leap, the risks barely averted at every turn.

I also invite everyone reading these pages to bring your idea to the surface. To find that part of yourself that will become the conduit of your own maker journey. To reach that place of excitement where you hit your flow and surrender to the people, places, and unexpected things that are drawn toward you and your purpose. Like Elliott, Jeff, Brett, and Jeremy, you can become a force to invent new things that will impact the world around us. I invite you to Make No Small Plans . . . so that you, too, can live your biggest life!

—*Jody Levy, global director and CEO, Summit*
Spring 2021

CONTENTS

MAKE NO SMALL PLANS

INTRODUCTION

We've all been told that big ideas are impossible. Start your sentence with "I know this sounds crazy, but I was thinking . . ." and you'll be cut off before you can even explain your vision and why it's revolutionary.

The purity of our dreams gets corrupted when it meets the reality of other people's experiences. "It's not going to work," they say. "It's not the right time." "We don't have the money." "Somebody else could do it better." And if it's not someone else shooting you down, we often do it to ourselves, dismissing our own ideas before even uttering them out loud. And yet most great businesses, products, and causes were deemed completely absurd and impractical notions at the outset.

We're here to tell you that there's never a bad time for a crazy idea. But there's also never a good time to start a business; we certainly didn't begin ours during one.

Summit Series was originally a conference series and a community of young, ambitious thinkers trying to begin their professional lives in the aftermath of the global financial crisis, both burdened by the instability of this new world and blessed with the opportunity to create something new in its wake. Over the coming decade, it would develop into a multi-disciplinary festival, attracting international leaders, pioneering entrepreneurs, and creative luminaries. But at the start, everyone told us we were crazy to dream that big.

In our early twenties, we lived in a house belonging to one of our grandmothers in a Florida retirement community, sleeping in bunk beds and on couches. Later that year, we were the first organization to connect a group of entrepreneurs to the Obama administration during a White House event focused on policy changes to support start-up founders. By our mid-twenties, we had chartered a fourteen-story ocean liner—the youngest people in history to do so, we'd later learn—and created our own floating city for a weekend. Before we turned thirty, we had bought North America's largest ski resort, Powder Mountain, on ten thousand acres of pristine Utah wilderness, and began turning it into a permanent home for our community.

How did four young dreamers with zero relationships, zero experience, and two college degrees between the four of us quickly rise to hosting luminaries like Richard Branson and Quincy Jones? We are not billionaires. We hold no patents. We are not geniuses or household names. We are simply four friends: Elliott, Jeff, Brett, and Jeremy.

Some people are destined to invent. To invest. To run for office. We have always had the burning desire to create impactful gatherings and build a community of entrepreneurs, creatives, and makers. We wanted to introduce them to new ideas. To inspire them. To help them succeed.

Historically, if you were a young writer or editor after World War I, you knew you could find Ernest Hemingway, F. Scott Fitzgerald, James Joyce, and Gertrude Stein at the

Ritz in Paris. If you were a young musician in the sixties, you knew that Diana Ross, Stevie Wonder, and Marvin Gaye were setting the world ablaze from Motown's offices on West Grand Boulevard in Detroit. And if you were a young entrepreneur in the decade of innovation that emerged from the rubble left by the greatest recession in a generation, you knew that the people at the heart of that revolution could be found at Summit Series.

The strength of our organization stems not from its four founders but from the hands of the remarkable community, connected by a common, insatiable desire to create, to share, and to nourish their best selves. Summit Series simply gives them a place to gather, collaborate with one another, and expand their minds, ideas, and friendships.

Over the years, those creators included everyone from Amazon's Jeff Bezos to actor and founder of the billion-dollar Honest Company, Jessica Alba. Hundreds of thought leaders have imparted their wisdom, such as business titans like Mark Cuban and Ray Dalio, media mavericks like CNN founder Ted Turner, and mindfulness gurus like Ram Dass and Eckhart Tolle.

Our guests were as wide-reaching as former president Bill Clinton and Pulitzer Prize–winning musician Kendrick Lamar. From professor and author Brené Brown to National Farm Workers association co-founder Dolores Huerta. Organic food champion Alice Waters has shared a podium with the late NBA legend Kobe Bryant, along with former Google CEO Eric Schmidt. Futurist Ray Kurzweil has shared wisdom with our community, as has scientist Craig Venter.

We share these names not to name-drop but rather to highlight common themes that all of these people embody: Vision and drive. A hunger to improve society. An eagerness to inspire the same in others. And, with Summit Series, a platform from which to do it.

What you'll find in these pages is our origin story and meditations on the philosophies that helped us build our community and our company, despite setbacks and challenges.

The truth is, we had some bruising experiences along the way. Some of the pages that follow are embarrassing. But we want to be honest about who we *were*, and show you the hard lessons we had to endure in order to gain whatever wisdom we have today. We want to show people how not to stumble where we fell, and encourage them to build something great, even if—especially if—they have no idea what they are doing.

Although the ideas in this book are immensely valuable to each of us, we can't claim them as our own. We're not the smartest people in the room; we're simply the ones who put the room together.

We wrote *Make No Small Plans* to explain how we created this community despite the odds and, more importantly, to help others think bigger and accomplish more. Envisioning change isn't just for artists and start-up founders, after all. It's vital for teachers, nurses, mechanics, parents, and every one of us who wants to make the most of where we are, right now.

What follows is more than a story about four kids who were determined to dream big—it's the story of twenty thousand of some of the most interesting people alive coming together to improve the future of those who will follow them.

Not only did they teach us about building successful, iconic businesses; they also shared their most intimate life philosophies, dreams, and fears. Over the past ten years, we have absorbed the wisdom of these leaders, and now we want to pass that on to the next generation of leaders.

If there's one bedrock conviction underlying everything we do, it's that the world needs more big thinking—and needs it right now. It needs more seekers, dreamers, risk-takers, and doers. Don't wait for the "right" moment to take that leap; if you do, it might never come. And the world doesn't have time for that. We need people dreaming crazy ideas and pushing past their reservations. Now like never before, we need to be radical creators, to protect the planet and to do exponentially more good.

The world is too big for small plans. So make yours accordingly.

1

THERE'S NO BETTER BUILDING BLOCK THAN TRUST

If you were thinking about starting a company back in 2007, it's safe to say we wouldn't have been your first-round draft picks.

Elliott Bisnow was a socially awkward twenty-two-year-old living in his childhood bedroom who'd dropped out of college to sell ads for his dad's online newsletter.

Brett Leve was working on commission at a real estate brokerage firm just as the housing bubble burst.

Jeff Rosenthal was frustrated in an associate position at Macy's, while attempting to create start-ups from a cramped shoebox apartment under a Manhattan highway on-ramp.

And Jeremy Schwartz was playing in a punk rock band named after a science fiction novel and touring the country, living on $8 a day.

We weren't exactly the Beatles. However, like many of our favorite bands who came together serendipitously, our story didn't happen overnight.

And it all started with Elliott.

He had just dropped out of the University of Wisconsin—the only college to accept him out of the seven to which he'd applied. Not that he wasn't smart. He just had his priorities in his own order. For example, one day as his sophomore finals approached, he headed to a study group with his girlfriend. While she took her studies seriously, he spent more time thinking about starting a business than he did attending class. But finals were finals, so he promised he'd join her study group for the cram session.

They stepped into the hush of the Helen C. White Library, where everyone in the group reached into their backpacks and quietly unloaded stacks of books onto the solid wood table. Elliott, however, pulled out a copy of *The Wall Street Journal* instead. The others looked at him like he was joking, but he began to read in earnest. After finishing the front page, he flipped to the next one, and a silence-shattering crinkle reverberated through the hall. Every head over every table lifted and turned.

"What are you *doing*?" Elliott's girlfriend whispered.

"I'm studying the world."

"This is the time to study for *exams*."

"But I need to learn about business. I heard that if I read *The Wall Street Journal* every day, I can learn how business works."

Her eyes closed and she slowly shook her head. The relationship wouldn't last, but Elliott's interest in the mechanics of the outside world would. It seemed to Elliott that everybody in college was working on the same problems that had already been solved by students the year before, and others the year before that. But Elliott didn't want to solve his professors' problems. He had his own problems to figure out.

During his freshman and sophomore years, he'd tried to

start a T-shirt business that failed to sell any T-shirts. Then he tried to start a creative consulting firm that never attracted a single client. After his sophomore year, he went home to Washington, D.C., and got a commission-only job selling ads for his dad's online real estate newsletter. He was terrible at it to start. But that hadn't deterred him in the past.

For instance, Elliott had started playing tennis at age twelve, years after many other kids got their first lesson. He was so hopelessly behind in the beginning that he lost most of his matches for the first four years. Determined to get better, he played for five hours a day, every day, eventually working his way up to ranking in the top thirty-five amateur players in his age division nationwide. He even received a tennis scholarship to college.

Now, he figured, he just needed to apply the same level of perseverance to being a salesperson.

After a few steakhouse lunches, he got lucky and made a couple of sales. From there, he identified three hundred companies to pitch, typed their contact information into a spreadsheet, and took the list back to school for his junior year so he could make calls from his college apartment.

As it turned out, selling local real estate ads was a lot tougher from 850 miles away. The distance gave him his first appreciation for the value of face-to-face connection. Cold calls could open doors—but then he needed to walk through those doors, shake hands with someone, and get to know them to close the deal. Over that semester, he managed to make a few successful sales, and he finally got his first check in the mail. The way Elliott saw it, the reason everyone went to college was to get a job. Holding that check in his hand, he realized he *had* a job.

When he went home for winter break, Elliott decided to

take a semester off to see how he would fare working full-time with his dad. He attended every networking event in the D.C. metro area to drum up leads. He eventually met a young twentysomething who had the innate ability to connect and easily relate to all kinds of people: Brett Leve.

Brett had grown up in the suburbs of Boston. His dad owned gas stations and was the type of business owner who would personally empty the ATM machines at his business. Brett pumped gas and made sandwiches for pocket money as a kid, but a summer job after he graduated high school changed his outlook on working.

He'd received an advertisement in the mail about selling Cutco knives to family and friends. He learned the pitch and can still recite it to this day: "American-made. Full resin handle. Five-A medical-grade stainless steel. Guaranteed forever, not just in your lifetime; you can pass them on. Your kids can call us and we'll sharpen them forever."

Brett sold $50,000 worth of knives in a single summer. At eighteen years old, he ranked fifty-second out of eight thousand sales reps across America. The lessons he learned during those few months would eventually help save our company years down the road.

Back then, Brett saw the money he earned as a means to travel—to get away from the gas station aisles he grew up in. He enrolled at George Washington University in D.C. and started throwing college parties at local clubs. After he graduated, he took a job working for commissions at a real estate brokerage firm. Normally that would've been a great way to learn the building blocks of land development—if not for the timing. The gears of the housing market ground to a halt in the run-up to the global financial crisis. With no deals to be made Brett was forced to pay his bills by continuing to throw college parties around the George Washington campus. Which, coincidentally, is how he met Jeff Rosenthal.

Jeff grew up in Dallas, Texas, and moved to Washington, D.C., to study international business at American University with a soccer scholarship.

His childhood was shaped by his grandfather's philosophy: "A large extended family is the greatest luxury in life." His grandmother Joy—all four feet eleven inches of her—was the matriarch of the family. She held seventy cousins, aunts, and uncles together by hosting family dinners nearly every weekend. Jeff also grew up with learning differences. His ADHD precipitated his bouncing between schools for most of his youth, and he never felt like he fit in.

Growing up, Jeff had been a goalkeeper for elite soccer clubs. His team competed for national championships, and he was admitted to IMG Academy in Bradenton, Florida, a school that develops players for the U.S. National Team, as well as hundreds of pro athletes in a wide variety of sports.

His dreams were stopped short—literally—when he stopped growing. He watched as bigger, more athletic players saved more goals than he ever could.

Because he couldn't get much playing time in college, he quit the team sophomore year. For the first time in his life, he was left with an abundance of free time. He began making friends outside of sports, many of whom had come to study in D.C. from around the world; this had a profound effect on Jeff's worldview, personality, and interests.

His new free time led him to take an internship with Congress, which turned into a full-time job as a floor staffer and congressional wrangler for the Rules Committee in the U.S. House of Representatives.

Around this time, Jeff's entrepreneurial qualities emerged.

He started an online vintage clothing company that did moderately well, and began to throw parties for his AU classmates, which is how he met Brett. Years of competition and exposure to a championship team culture had taught Jeff that players sharpen each other like swords. The camaraderie and shared aspirations of a team create a feedback loop where members have to continuously better themselves—and each other—in order to be exceptional.

This created a problem for Jeff once he was no longer on a team. Without a crew around him, Jeff found it difficult to motivate himself.

He spent close to a year traveling the world, spending what little money he had from his college ventures. Afterward, he moved to New York City, rented a tiny apartment, buoyed a couple of small start-ups, and took an entry-level job as a junior buyer at Macy's, just as the economy faltered and all of retail shuddered.

Without realizing it yet, Jeff was a player in need of a team as much as we were a team in need of players.

Our fourth member, Jeremy Schwartz, was Brett Leve's closest friend from high school. While he wasn't a natural salesperson like the rest of us, Jeremy brought his own unique and much-needed skill set to the group.

His band was named Ice Nine Kills, after a substance in the Kurt Vonnegut novel *Cat's Cradle*. The group sold out shows across the United States, became popular using guerrilla marketing tactics on social networking websites such as MySpace, and snuck their way onto the Warped Tour, which was America's largest traveling music festival at the time. Fans went so far as to tattoo Jeremy's song lyrics on their arms.

The band had built a loyal national following and were

selling out major venues coast to coast. Touring would've been a beautiful way for a young man to live out his passion—if Jeremy didn't have to do it on $8 a day.

Illegal music downloads were proliferating. The record industry was in shambles. Major labels were consolidating. The only money the group made was from touring, CDs, and merch sales. Fans offered up their homes as crash pads. They were so supportive that when the band's van broke down, they housed and fed the musicians for the two weeks it was in the shop.

Jeremy loved performing and was at one with the band's loyal community. But the grind of touring nine months out of the year was taking a toll. Despite the band's growing success and popularity, Jeremy decided the lifestyle wasn't for him. Brett offered him a different path, so he parted ways with his band and joined us.

Our destiny was to build a community—to support a scene of entrepreneurs that would come to define a generation of world-changing businesses. But at the time, we were all just looking for friendship. We were a crew of college dropouts and eccentric creatives who found solace in supporting each other's wildest ideas. And we figured there must be more of us out there.

So we decided to take a risk. And then we kept on taking that risk again, and again, and again. We repeatedly pushed all our chips into the center of the table, and each time the wins outweighed the numerous losses.

That didn't make it easy, though. Bold ideas challenge our identities. They threaten what we have and what we know. We don't trust them, not because they break the rules but because they create new ones of their own.

But the Great Recession had shredded the old playbooks,

along with the stock market, and we saw a space emerging where a new trail could be blazed. Take any public figure you admire and chances are they reached success by pursuing a bold and disruptive path—by hatching a crazy idea and sticking with it.

Elliott was the first of us to dream that big.

2

YOUR REACH SHOULD ALWAYS EXCEED YOUR GRASP

Elliott may have had a dream, but that didn't mean that he had any idea of what he was doing. In 2006, a year before Elliott and Brett would first meet, Elliott finally decided to drop out of college to join his dad's business selling real estate ads full-time. He had a few early successes closing deals, and figured that he was going to learn more from chatting to businesspeople back in D.C. than from his introductory economics classes in Wisconsin.

Night after night he headed off to events filled with strangers without really understanding how to engage them. Elliott viewed every handshake as a new prospect to convert into ad sales. But with enthusiasm as his only tool, he could come across as a little too eager.

"Hi, I'm Elliott from Bisnow on Business. I just wanted to say hello! What do you do?"

"Hi, I'm Elliott from Bisnow on Business. Great to meet you! Are you looking for more exposure for your company?"

"Hi, I'm Elliott from Bisnow on Business. Loving that shirt! What are you working on currently?"

People who loved him began to call him "Casino-Floor Elliott"; those who didn't coined less endearing terms. But his persistence paid off, and late in the evening he'd return to his tiny rented office across from the White House and enter the business cards he'd gathered into his company's database. Then, instead of trekking back to his parents' house on a cul-de-sac in D.C., where he still lived, he'd often crash on some seat cushions placed under his desk.

While his college friends were out partying in Wisconsin, contemplating their first internships, and deciding on their major, Elliott would wake up in that shabby office and spend much of his day cold-calling potential clients. Elliott had intentionally rented his office space a hundred yards from the White House so he could tell people he was in the center of the action—even if getting to his office meant riding up a creaky elevator and walking past other offices with windows looking into alleys on his way to his own office, which didn't have a window at all.

He'd pick up the phone and open with "Yes, I'm calling from next to the White House" to try to impress clients. It didn't work. Nor did cold-calling the other tenants in the building to try to sell them advertising. Eventually, the building's general manager intervened. "Stop cold-calling our tenants," he warned Elliott. "Also, I know you're sleeping under your desk at night. Stop that, too."

The landlord had figured out that Elliott was crashing in the building because one night, after a Casino-Floor Elliott session, he got locked out of his office—in his boxers and T-shirt. He couldn't figure out how to get back in, so he had to ask a night manager at the front desk to open the door so he could get back to the safety and comfort of his shoes and pants.

Elliott was making *some* sales, however, and he was happy to be building a business with his dad. But the grind felt meaningless, and it made him wonder if this was what he'd been put on the planet to do.

The truth was, Elliott had no idea what he wanted to do. He'd met plenty of salespeople and real estate agents since dropping out of school twelve months prior, but aside from his dad, he didn't know a single person who had started a business.

He wanted to meet somebody wired like he was, but more experienced. Someone who could show him the way. That person wasn't knocking on the door of his small office—even if it was "next to the White House."

Snow was falling at the end of 2007 when Elliott heard of relationships being formed on chairlifts and deals being made over après-ski drinks. He realized that networking opportunities weren't restricted to city streets—they could take place on ski slopes as well.

Elliott had an idea. His aunt and uncle lived not far from a ski resort in Utah, and he'd vacationed there growing up. Maybe it was time to pay them a visit.

The childhood dresser where Elliott used to put away his clothes was now filled with thousands of business cards. He decided to tap into his network and invite a group of people to the mountains in the hopes of getting to know some of them. If he selected the right twenty people, perhaps he could establish seven or eight friendships, and those new friends could show him the way. (And if he made some ad sales out of it, even better.)

He turned to a fresh page in a spiral notepad and wrote:

"The Best of the Best." He listed twenty people he was on good terms with whom he thought he might be able to learn from. The list included a real estate broker, a furniture salesperson, a manager at a construction company, a host at a local restaurant, an insurance risk analyst at AIG, and a college graduate who'd just taken a job at AARP.

Elliott emailed them his pitch: "I'm an entrepreneur. I really want to bring together twenty creative people and build a peer group so that we can connect with each other, meet new friends, and brainstorm. I don't know most of you that well. What if we went off to a ski retreat in Utah for a weekend to really connect?"

Then he called them one by one to see if they'd be interested.

"Why would I go on a ski trip with twenty people I don't know?" the first invitee said.

"Not a good idea," said another.

"My next vacation is in six months," said the third. "I'm gonna go with *my* friends. I don't want to meet *your* friends, who, it seems, *you* don't even really know that well."

Elliott drew lines through the names of everyone who said no. But he didn't give up. He kept reaching for his phone. The lawyer wanted to know why he should meet the furniture guy. The furniture guy wanted to know why he should hang out with the insurance risk analyst.

There seemed to be some interest on the next call, with the real estate broker.

"When's the trip?" he asked.

"April 17."

"April 17? That's a terrible time for a ski trip!"

"It's not about the skiing!"

"So, you want me to go with all these random people I'm

not interested in? Why don't you come by my office instead? We can chat about real estate brokerage."

"I don't want to chat about real estate brokerage!" Elliott said. "I want to meet other entrepreneurs!"

Elliott continued to cross off names as he went down the list, and the further down he got, the more adamant the responses became. But he kept on calling.

"You don't even know how to plan a trip," said the next. "I know you; you can't even sell ads! How am I going to trust you to plan my vacation?"

Another line through another name.

Finally, Elliott reached the last person on the list after days of trying.

"Come on," Elliott said, "I've called you twenty times to ask you if you wanted to go on my ski trip."

"If I wanted to go, I would've called you back."

The last name on his pad was crossed off.

Not a single yes. And still Elliott believed in his idea. He wasn't bothered by rejection. After all, he made cold calls for a living.

Thanks to all his years as a lousy tennis player with a dedication to the grind, Elliott processed losses differently than most other people. When he reviewed the avalanche of nos on his pad, he had an epiphany: No one he reached out to thought his idea was interesting enough. He was thinking too small, and his intuition now pointed him toward something much larger.

Summit Series was born the moment Elliott realized he needed a more inspiring list of names.

3

READY, FIRE, AIM

Sometimes you can have the right idea and pitch it to the wrong person.

The names on the business cards gathering dust in Elliott's childhood dresser were valuable if you were selling insurance or couches. But Elliott wasn't aspiring to be a furniture salesperson. Which people, Elliott wondered, did he *really* wish he could spend time with and learn from? He started to think about the companies that inspired him and the new generation of entrepreneurs behind them.

He put down the spiral notepad, turned on his computer, and created a new spreadsheet. He searched for people his own age who had seemingly created something out of nothing. The names at the top of the list included:

BLAKE MYCOSKIE: Blake had invented an entirely new way of looking at business with TOMS Shoes. With every pair sold, TOMS gave a pair of shoes to a child in need.

RICKY VAN VEEN AND JOSH ABRAMSON: In addition to starting Vimeo, one of the world's biggest video sites, Ricky and Josh assembled the

world's largest repository of jokes and funny videos as founders of
the website CollegeHumor.

JOEL HOLLAND: Joel had landed on *Business Week's* "25 Under 25"
list after he traveled around the country as a teenager filming
video clips of skylines and city landmarks. The video service he
founded, VideoBlocks, saved companies thousands of dollars in
fees that were being charged by traditional competitors for stock
footage. And he was still in college.

These were the types of people Elliott related to and
wanted to learn from—and he figured they might be able to
learn something from each other, too.

Joel Holland was Elliott's first call. Elliott sensed if he
could get Joel to come to Utah, it would make the calls that
followed easier. By confirming someone on the "25 Under 25"
list, he would validate the trip and incentivize others to join.

Elliott first reached out to Joel shortly after *Business
Week*'s list appeared. But Joel was naturally receiving lots of
calls at the time—and ignoring most of them. If the calls
were truly important, Joel figured, the callers would try
again. Elliott called a second time, and again Joel didn't pick
up. But after Elliott bombarded him with Facebook messages, Joel finally gave in.

When they met over lunch, Elliott pitched him his far-
fetched idea: to bring together a bunch of young, committed
company founders—whom he didn't know, and who didn't
know each other—on a mountain, to discuss professional
challenges facing their businesses and find collaborative solutions.

Joel wasn't sold. He told Elliott that entrepreneurs tend
to be motivated by their singular visions. America's love of
individualism tended to outweigh the sacrifice required for
the greater good. He was a no.

So Elliott turned to the next names on his list: the founders of CollegeHumor.

Childhood friends Ricky Van Veen and Josh Abramson had started their company in 1999 while studying at different colleges. Elliott had been captivated by one of their videos and watched it on repeat in his college dorm. Ricky and Josh also caught his attention because, back in the nineties, college students rarely started their own businesses. (Oh, how times have changed.) Elliott dreamed of doing everything that Ricky and Josh were doing.

By the time he called them, CollegeHumor had grown to about fifty employees and moved into a loft-like headquarters in lower Manhattan. Their assistant refused to let Elliott's calls go through time and again, but Elliott kept trying. Finally, in exasperation, the assistant passed him on to Josh.

Elliott gave him the pitch. Josh thought he was a lunatic and that the ski trip would be a disaster. Why would he fly all the way to Utah with this kid from "next to the White House"? But Josh's company *was* founded upon humor, and he couldn't resist the opportunity to play a prank on his unsuspecting co-founder. He told Elliott he thought the ski trip was a *brilliant* idea, gave him Ricky's cellphone number, and encouraged Elliott to call.

When Ricky answered the phone, he thought Elliott was trying to sell him a time-share at a ski resort. But there was one line in Elliott's pitch that he just couldn't wave aside: Elliott was offering first-class airline tickets to Utah. Ricky and Josh had been written up in *The New Yorker,* but they'd never flown first-class. Ricky was curious.

Who was this guy, Elliott Bisnow? Nobody threw conferences or retreats for entrepreneurs in their twenties and thirties; the best they were getting in New York was an overstuffed happy hour in a lavish loft downtown. Was this a scam?

They figured there was only one way to find out. Entrepreneurs tend to have a higher tolerance for risk—and this one came with cushy plane tickets. Ricky was curious about Elliott because, unlike the people on Elliott's original list, Ricky had no clue who Elliott was. He walked over to Josh's office with a question.

"Doesn't Ben Lerer have a house in Park City, Utah?"

Ben was a friend of theirs who had started a website covering food, drink, travel, and entertainment, called Thrillist.

"Yeah, Ben *does* have a house there," Josh responded warily, realizing his prank had backfired and Ricky was now actually interested.

Ricky figured that if they went on this ski trip and it was a hoax, they'd at least have first-class tickets to fly out and see Ben. Plus, they could ask this overenthusiastic character to invite Ben on the ski trip, so they'd have safety in numbers.

And just like that, Elliott had his first two guests locked in. Not only that, but he had one of New York's rising young entrepreneurs thrown in for free.

Except it wasn't free. Not for Elliott. He had no idea how much all of this was going to cost. He hadn't priced out the first-class airfares, or figured out how he was going to afford the accommodations, dinners, and ski passes he was promising. He didn't have a budget—but he did have some credit cards.

Elliott doubled back to Joel Holland. But instead of asking him to fully commit, he posed a different question, one that would later become the bedrock of Summit Series's strategy for growth: Elliott asked him if there was anybody *else* he knew who might like to come.

Joel threw out a few names and vouched for them. As he did, he began to wonder: *If I'm suggesting that my friends go on this wild, all-expenses-paid ski trip . . . why am I not going with them?*

So Joel was all in.

That was the moment Elliott knew. If he could get four yeses, he could get twenty. There's a critical tipping point of momentum for anything in the world, whether it's physics or business. Getting the initial traction is the most difficult part, but once things are moving, it gets easier and easier.

Next, Elliott reached out to Blake Mycoskie at TOMS. Elliott had been fascinated with TOMS ever since college, when he'd first read about them and immediately bought a pair of their shoes.

The company had a simple backstory. During a trip to Argentina, Blake had noticed that many children weren't wearing shoes. But instead of just buying a pair for the kids he met, he wanted to find a more sustainable, long-term solution. He decided to work with a local cobbler to make traditional Argentine *alpargatas* that could be sold in the United States to subsidize footwear for those who didn't have any. When a *Los Angeles Times* reporter wrote a story about TOMS after the first pairs appeared in a boutique, Blake was immediately overwhelmed with fourteen times as many orders as his available stock. He could barely keep up. TOMS would go on to give away more than a hundred million pairs of shoes.

But back then, Elliott was curious about how Blake would scale a company built on such a humble business model. So he called Blake's rickety old warehouse in Santa Monica. Fortunately for Elliott, Blake's assistant appreciated his optimism and persistence. After multiple checks to confirm the trip wasn't a scheme, the assistant passed along the invitation to Blake, emphasizing that it was all-expenses-paid: "Worst-case scenario, you'll get a free weekend of skiing out of it."

Blake was intrigued enough to take the call. He listened attentively, then ultimately asked the same question that everybody else had asked: "Who else is going on the trip?"

Elliott rattled off the names. "Joel Holland from *Business Week*'s '25 Under 25' list, Ricky Van Veen and Josh Abramson from CollegeHumor, Thrillist founder Ben Lerer . . ."

Blake was in.

Now Elliott had to figure out a way to pay for it all. Though he still had no idea how much it would cost him, he knew it would be smart to try to get sponsors to cover his losses. So he started making calls.

He knew a guy named Steve who had been a volunteer football coach for his brother in high school and now had an entry-level job as a broker at commercial real estate giant Jones Lang LaSalle. He begged him to use every connection at the company to convince them to put up some money. "You could meet some good clients on this trip, Steve," Elliott pitched, trying to bite back the desperation in his voice. "What if your firm put up $10,000 as a sponsor?" Then he held his breath.

He didn't realize just how good that opportunity might have sounded to Steve. It put an entry-level broker trying to drum up business in the position to pitch a creative idea to his boss. Luckily for both of them, Steve's manager saw the upside, and the company put up $10,000.

Now Elliott realized he wasn't selling a ski trip—he was selling a new business opportunity. Who else, Elliott wondered, would want to be around the next generation of business leaders? The answer became clear to him: venture capitalists. He rustled through his stack of business cards and called a contact at a VC firm he'd met just once. "This trip is a great opportunity to get leads," he promised. "And you'll never guess who else will be there."

After some wooing, it worked. The VC firm decided to toss in $10,000 as well.

Ideas for other sponsors began to click. It dawned on Elliott that his ski gear was seven years old. What if he could get some new winter apparel for everyone? He cold-called a marketing manager at The North Face and boldly asked: "Are you interested in changing the trajectory of your brand forever?" To Elliott's surprise, they actually *were* interested. It turned out that they liked the idea of marketing to a new generation of entrepreneurs. That and Elliott's ask was actually quite small by their standard. North Face came through with twenty jackets and twenty travel bags.

Then he contacted *Fortune*. He figured a media sponsor would really give his event some credibility. The magazine declined to give him sponsorship money, but one of their editors was intrigued by the idea and decided to have a reporter call with questions.

Elliott had solved his first problem: getting twenty busy people to come skiing with him. He'd even nearly solved his second problem: The entire event would add up to about $38,000, and Elliott had recouped roughly $30,000 in sponsorships. His credit cards could shoulder the rest.

But he had no idea that his solutions had snowballed into a whole new set of problems.

To start, where would they all sleep? Airbnb was nearly a year away from its launch, and regardless, Elliott had never rented a home before in his life. He'd lived in dorm rooms in college, and now he was back living with his parents (when he wasn't sneakily sleeping under his desk). In fact, the only vacations Elliott had ever been on up to this point had been family trips. That meant he'd never booked a hotel room. He'd never made a dinner reservation at a restaurant. He'd never even purchased any alcohol, because he didn't drink.

He needed help, so he called in the cavalry: his mother, Margot. As the parent who had brought all of his childhood holidays to life, she came to the rescue, as mothers often do, and found a ski house at Alta Ski Area in Utah. There was just one issue: The home she rented had only nine bedrooms. Elliott had nearly twenty guests coming. He was going to have to ask nearly two dozen strangers to share rooms.

Still, there was an even bigger problem. Elliott had absolutely no idea how to throw a party.

4

AUTHENTICITY TRUMPS PERFECTION

Elliott landed in Salt Lake City on a crisp, clear Friday afternoon in April 2008—only two hours ahead of his guests. He rented a Suburban and raced to a convenience store to pick up some snacks for their arrival, and proudly bought beer for the first time in his life.

Everything seemed set as he arrived at the house to unpack. He now had a case of beer in the refrigerator and what seemed like a mountain of snacks on the table. And it *was* a mountain of snacks—for one person. *We'll probably have beer one night this weekend,* he imagined, *and everyone will have one.*

As guests began to trickle in, Elliott graciously gave a tour of the rental home to each new person who arrived.

"There are no plans for this weekend," Elliott told Joel Holland as they headed for the kitchen. "The idea is for everybody to get to know each other. The entire weekend is one big party!"

Elliott proudly swung open the door of the refrigerator to reveal twenty-four cans of beer.

One case of beer? For twenty people? This, Joel thought, *is going to be one hell of a party.*

With beer having historically proven itself to be a wonderful social lubricant for young people in uncomfortable settings, those twenty-four cans disappeared almost immediately once the guests found out they'd be sharing rooms with people they didn't know.

All anybody could feel at this point was a deep sense of awkwardness.

Things only got more uncomfortable when an artist Elliott had invited showed up. He had asked the painter to showcase his canvases, thinking that the display would add some creative energy to the group. Tempted by the prospect of making sales to a collection of highly successful entrepreneurs, the artist had transported his life's work to the event in a U-Haul. At the time, most of the young entrepreneurs were completely focused on their businesses, and while they were wealthy in start-up stock, not one of them had ever bought art, nor had the slightest interest in purchasing any on this trip. After the artist unveiled his creations, he eagerly moved throughout the room, seeking sales, while all the entrepreneurs deftly looked for ways to avoid him. They opened their laptops at a long table, because "having to get some work done" felt like a reasonable excuse. "Going out on a beer run" also did the trick—and eased the rapidly snowballing tension.

Ricky and Josh from CollegeHumor immediately zeroed in on all the discomfort and decided it would be fun to create some more. When the group piled into a few cars and headed to the upscale restaurant Elliott's mother had scouted out for dinner, Ricky and Josh were already hatching a plot.

The group convened around a long table, with Elliott positioned at the head. When Elliott got up to go to the bathroom, Ricky and Josh quickly told everyone their plan: They would hand the maître d' a white card to place in front of Elliott when he sat back down. They asked the rest of the group to play along.

Elliott returned to the table and took his seat, and the maître d' gave an award-winning performance. "So sorry," he said remorsefully, delicately placing the note in front of Elliott. He was so sincere that it was obvious there was a problem.

"Elliott, what's that?" Josh pried.

"I just got the weirdest card."

"What does it say?"

Your attire is not appropriate to the standards of the club, and we ask that you change immediately.

—Management

"Oh man, you need to go change," someone called out.

"I don't have extra clothes in the car!"

"Well, where's the closest store you can buy some?"

"I don't know."

"But you *have* to change."

"What's wrong with my clothes?"

"Look at your shirt. It's not appropriate."

"It's a button-down shirt. The same kind as *you're* wearing."

"It's *not* the same. Look at the *color* of your shirt!"

This went on until every inch of Elliott's attire had been

thoroughly dissected down to the contour of his collar. Elliott's frustration mounted until everyone burst into laughter.

Elliott shut his eyes and gave a reluctant smile. Then he began to laugh along with the table. In that moment, all the tension that had been accumulating from the time everyone arrived was released. Lively conversations sprang up around the table, and everyone began to relax into the evening and connect on a deeper level. At the end of dinner, everyone was in a jovial mood, and far too many people crammed into the back of Elliott's Suburban for the trip home.

It was dark when Elliott began driving the rowdy crew back, and there were no other cars on the road. He approached a sign that read NO LEFT TURN. But because the road was completely empty, and the home Elliott had rented was to the left, he took the turn. As soon as he did, a siren pierced the darkness. A police car had been in hiding, and it pulled behind the rental car as Elliott rolled the overstuffed vehicle to a stop.

The patrol officer sat inside his cruiser for an excruciatingly long time. Ben Lerer seized the moment.

"Bisnow, you're going to jail! Your event is over! And it's never even started!"

"Stop! I didn't do anything wrong!"

"Yes, you did. We're crammed in here like sardines. We're illegally sitting in the back!"

Elliott was eyeing the patrol car in the rear-view mirror, nearly obscured by the nine people in the back seats.

"Stop it, Ben!"

The tension in Elliott's voice was an open invitation for *everybody* in the Suburban to pile on.

"You shouldn't have been drinking, Elliott!"

"I don't drink!"

"You're going to jail! It's Friday night—you'll be there all weekend. But don't worry. I'll drive the car, take over the house, and run your event!"

Everybody in the car was howling at Elliott just as the officer exited the cruiser.

"Shut up, Ben! Please!"

Laughter was almost bursting through the closed windows as Elliott's heart pounded and the officer approached the door. And then, suddenly, there was a respectful, almost cinematic silence.

Elliott rolled down his window. The officer took his driver's license and registration, peered suspiciously into the back of the vehicle, and then walked back to the cruiser. Elliott felt like he was being investigated for an hour, and the guys in the back seats used every traumatic second of it to heap more comic abuse on him. Finally the officer returned and calmly extended a ticket, as he would have to anyone else.

Once Elliott's window was back up, the heckling flared up again and followed Elliott all the way home. It was an initiation that was a better bonding experience than anything Elliott could've planned. Nobody minded sharing a bedroom with others after that. There was so much to rehash and laugh about, most of it at Elliott's willing expense. It felt like summer camp, except with more snow and less poison ivy.

The next day, everyone hit the slopes. Sam Altman, the future president of Y Combinator, and the founders of Vimeo and TOMS were hanging out and swapping stories of their struggles. They were learning about each other's best business practices and how they balanced work with their personal lives. Each shed light on past failures and what could be learned from them. By the end of the weekend, everybody was familiar with everyone else's businesses and the stories that made them. Some of the guests had even begun lifelong friendships.

But perhaps Elliott had learned the biggest lesson of all. So many people are frightened to throw an event, set up a meeting, or even send an important email unless it's perfectly crafted—as if you shouldn't put yourself out there unless everything is flawless.

Elliott understood in that moment that the most important quality an event can have is space for the unplanned—room for the spontaneity and randomness that create sparks. It's the difference between a highly polished apple you get in the supermarket and the slightly bruised organic one that's fallen from a tree. Brush it off, and the roadside apple tastes infinitely better.

Just as Elliott had relentlessly picked up the phone to call people, he'd followed through and thrown an event that even his friends thought he was crazy to attempt to host—and now he had twenty new friends who didn't think he was crazy at all.

In fact, they actually kind of liked him.

As his guests left the mountain, they asked Elliott if he'd assemble another get-together for everyone six months down the road. The idea had never even occurred to him; he'd barely managed to pull a single weekend off, and it would take him months to pay down his credit card debt. After he said goodbye to the crew, he soon got a phone call from the *Fortune* reporter asking how things went. As the call was wrapping up, the reporter posed one final question.

"So, what's your event called?" the reporter asked.

It didn't occur to Elliott to have a name for the ski trip.

Why would he give the trip a name? He didn't have a name for hanging out with friends on the weekend, so how was this any different?

"What do you mean?" he asked.

"You organized an event. What's the name of it?"

"Right. Of course it has a name . . ."

"Well, what is it?"

Elliott glanced at the North Face jacket he was still wearing from the weekend and read the words right off the sleeve.

"Summit Series."

5

REPLACE YOUR WEAKNESSES WITH A PARTNER'S STRENGTHS

Suddenly people were returning Elliott's calls.

Apparently, you get a warmer welcome when you actually have a track record of flying people first-class, introducing them to people they wished they could meet, and hosting them for an exciting weekend, all expenses paid.

After hearing how amazing the ski trip was, those who'd declined Elliott's first invitation wondered what they'd missed. They apologized, left him voice messages, and asked him when he'd be organizing the next one. And where? The snow was melting in the mountains, after all, and a year seemed like a long time to wait.

So Elliott decided to swap the snowboards for board shorts as he started dreaming up the next event. Sixty promising entrepreneurs. Six months down the road. Sunny Mexico.

He could practically feel the sun on his back just thinking about it: a long weekend spent trading business tips, while his guests sipped margaritas by the pool and swam with *tor-*

tugas. It was a welcome daydream—he was still living with his parents in his childhood bedroom and working in an office with no natural sunlight.

Elliott also couldn't afford to take time off work—that credit card debt wasn't going to pay itself off—and he wasn't going to ask his mother to scout the location for him a second time. But a friend who was feeling stifled by his corporate job leapt at the opportunity to help.

Ryan Begelman was working in a prestigious private equity firm in D.C. Most of his job focused on buying and trading real estate, but part of the position entailed downsizing companies that had been purchased in large acquisitions. In other words, he fired people.

After several years, Ryan grew tired of crunching spreadsheets all day in an uncomfortable suit. So, unbeknownst to his boss, he began looking at small real estate projects to buy in the D.C. area. He figured it might be his way out.

Eager to learn the local real estate market, he discovered a witty email newsletter about local real estate produced by Bisnow on Business. He became obsessed with it. With the desire to meet the newsletter's creators, Ryan tracked down Elliott at a real estate networking event, and cornered him on a rooftop overlooking the D.C. skyline. Upon meeting Elliott, Ryan was blown away. *Who is this kid? Two years younger than me and already living my dream of being an entrepreneur.*

Ryan started going to Elliott's office daily to talk business ideas and learn how Bisnow on Business worked. The two became fast friends, so when Elliott reached out to Ryan asking for help planning the Mexico event, he was happy to plug in.

Ryan was a skillful planner and organizer. He hit the

phones, calling every resort in Mexico to figure out a location and accommodations that wouldn't bust the bank.

He chose a location near Cancún. It seemed like an exciting getaway, and Cancún had direct flights from most major cities. Within a few hours, attendees could be on a white-sand beach surrounded by crystalline water. He found a hotel at Playa del Carmen that could accommodate everyone. It wasn't a five-star place—and yes, people would need to room together (again)—but Elliott had realized that intimacy was part of what made the first event so successful. Sharing rooms had created the summer-camp vibe that broke down barriers in snowy Utah.

With Ryan on board, Elliott no longer had to worry about logistics, something he wasn't very good at. That left Elliott with the time to do what he did best: cold-calling strangers.

The guests on the list he began putting together may not have known each other, but as post-dot-com business owners, they shared common aspirations and struggles. It was like the Ten Thousand Islands chain off the southwest coast of Florida: When you were on one of those islands, looking out at the expanse of water all around, you felt alone. But if you looked down from a great height, you would see how all those islands seemed to be linked in a chain.

Elliott's goal was to build a road that bridged all of these lonely islands. He wanted to show entrepreneurs who felt isolated how connected they actually were.

Facebook started in 2004. YouTube launched in 2005, Twitter in 2006. And the iPhone dropped in 2007. It was now the summer of 2008. Start-up culture was flourishing, and the Internet was allowing young people both in and out of college to market and sell their products online. With Summit Series, Elliott wanted each of those businesses to feel like they were connected to a burgeoning community, and that lessons learned by one could help lift another.

With all of Elliott's new connections, there wasn't a shortage of people to invite. His first list of names contained some of the brightest young business leaders in America.

TIM FERRISS: Tim published what became the modern manual for founders called *The 4-Hour Workweek* in 2007, and agreed to speak at the event in Mexico.

SCOTT HARRISON: Scott started Charity Water, a nonprofit that brings clean water to parched areas around the globe. He also agreed to give a talk.

CATHERINE LEVENE: Catherine ran DailyCandy, one of the most popular email newsletters in the United States, which would eventually be sold to Comcast for $125 million.

CHRIS SACCA: Chris jumped in even before he'd begun raising money for Lowercase Capital, which would become one of the most successful VC firms of all time.

GARRETT CAMP: Garrett would go on to co-found Uber.

CAROLINE MCCARTHY: Caroline would become a marketing strategist for Google, connecting the company with the most influential minds in social media.

TONY HSIEH: Tony was revolutionizing customer service over the Internet through the online retailer Zappos. A year after the Mexico event, he'd sell the company for a billion dollars.

Besides their obvious business accomplishments, the attendees possessed something even more meaningful: Each was driven by a passion, a powerful curiosity, and the will to succeed and push the world forward. This was the deeper bond that connected everyone. All of these entrepreneurs said yes. The more that other young business owners heard who was coming, the more momentum the list gained.

It wasn't all good news, though. Expenses for the Mexico trip were much higher than what Elliott had racked up in Utah. He knew that he could no longer afford to fly his guests to Mexico first-class, so the invitation let attendees know that it was up to them to get to Cancún. Once they arrived, however, everything would be covered. While the guys who heckled Elliott from the back of the Suburban in Park City couldn't resist poking fun at the disappearance of their first-class plane tickets, everyone understood that he couldn't fly in sixty guests internationally.

Even so, Elliott was going to have to raise roughly $130,000 in sponsorships to balance his costs—and he had to bring in this money while also working his day job. Fitting it all in was no easy task. He bounced between responding to emails about ad pixel dimensions, making cold calls to prospective new clients, and trying to confirm the attendance of the co-founder of Facebook. There was only so much time in a day, and he'd need some help selling sponsorships to the Mexico event.

Meanwhile, Ryan Begelman was cold-calling the ad agencies of Mercedes and Nike, trying to persuade them to contribute, and striking out left and right. That's when Ryan made a suggestion.

What about Brett Leve?

Of course. Brett Leve.

Elliott had first met Brett at an Urban Land Institute event that the two had attended to network. Elliott was there to gobble up business cards to help him sell more ads. Brett was there as a broker looking to meet people interested in developing real estate. But when the crowd that night filed into an adjacent room to listen to a lecture, the two of them were left alone at a table of crudités.

"Hi, I'm Elliott from Bisnow on Business!" Casino-Floor Elliott chirped. "Nice to meet you. Looks like you're the only other young person here."

"It does, doesn't it?" The casino vibe didn't really go over well with Brett.

"What do you do?" Elliott asked.

"I'm in real estate."

"Amazing!" Elliott said. "I'm in real estate, too! I have two seats to a Washington Nationals gala tomorrow night. You should come!"

Elliott assured him there were great connections to be made, and even though Brett felt something off-putting about Elliott, he couldn't help but be intrigued by his awkward exuberance. Something compelled him to say yes.

The following night, though, Brett didn't feel well. As he watched Elliott run circles around him snatching up business cards at the gala, he decided to leave. He thanked Elliott for the invitation, said goodbye, and headed home early.

"No worries," Elliott said, immediately pivoting to the person next to him. "Hi, I'm Elliott!"

Over time, Elliott continued to reach out to Brett. (In fact, Brett had even been one of the names on Elliott's original list of twenty local businesspeople. He had declined, just like the nineteen others.) Elliott eventually introduced him to Ryan, and it turned out that they lived a few blocks apart and went to the same gym. Brett and Ryan started to hang out every day and became close.

Less than a year later, after the successful Utah trip, Elliott felt confident he could handle the invite list for the Mexico event. He knew that Ryan could take care of logistics. What he needed was somebody who could make a party come to life and bring in sponsorship money.

Ryan reached out to Brett. "Remember that guy Elliott? Well, I'm spending a lot of time these days working with him," he said, "and I think you might want to get involved."

Brett hesitated. "Yeah, I'm not so sure about that guy."

"Look, he's . . . different," Ryan said. It was true. Elliott had spent nearly his entire adolescence obsessed with tennis and simply didn't know how to converse with people in a work setting. Brett, on the other hand, had casually learned social dynamics by selling knives and throwing parties in college. "But that's what makes a strong team, having people with different skills. You could really help us out."

Brett certainly knew everything Elliott didn't know about entertaining people. But he didn't want to help throw another party, as he did enough of that on weekends. If Brett was going to join, he was only interested in selling sponsorships. He figured if Elliott's concept didn't work out, he could at least use the sales opportunity to make some money for himself and also to make new connections that might benefit him down the line.

Brett met with Elliott and offered to bring in sponsorships on commission. To Brett, working on commission was not only the best indicator of people who are confident in their abilities and willingness to work, but not asking for a salary took all the defensiveness out of the negotiation.

The deal was done over a handshake. Brett would receive 20 percent of the money he brought in, and if that total exceeded $30,000, there'd be an opening for Brett to join as a partner.

It was not an easy time to sell sponsorships, though. Brett called every VC and law firm he could think of and only got two bites. After two months of work, he'd pulled in only $9,000.

Finally, things took a turn. Staples, the office supplies retailer, had just acquired a company called Corporate Express
as a way to expand its business into servicing corporate accounts. Brett's dad knew a guy at Staples who'd worked on
that acquisition, Jay Baitler.

Jay was the ideal referral. Brett knew he'd only have one
shot at convincing Jay to come on board, but Brett was ready.
In fact, he had been preparing for this call with Jay since he
was seven years old. Brett's work ethic had been forged at his
dad's gas stations. His dad worked six days a week, and took
off Sundays only because Brett's mom insisted. Brett figured
out early on that the best way to spend time with his dad was
to go to work with him. That put him on top of milk crates
behind the gas station counter when he was in second grade,
and over the years he scrubbed the bathrooms, pumped gas,
cleaned the bays, and grilled up steak-and-cheese sandwiches at the station's sub shop.

His extroverted nature worked well behind the counter
when he was young, and it worked even better years later
selling cutlery for Cutco. When he went off to college and
needed some cash in his pocket, Brett gravitated toward
throwing parties—basically selling college kids on the idea of
an unforgettable night. His style further evolved when he
graduated, fusing what he'd learned selling knives in high
school with what he'd picked up in college. He headed into
land development, convincing property developers to build
their condos on his boss's land.

In short, Brett had been selling one thing or another almost every day for nearly six years leading up to his call with
Jay Baitler, and he wasn't nervous in the least.

"Staples is a world-class brand," Brett said to start the
call, "and Corporate Express is an amazing acquisition. You

have billions of dollars in annual revenue." He explained how the workplace was changing, that millennials were growing organizations that rival the biggest companies in the world, and that some of the most influential members of this new generation of leaders were going to be at this Summit Series event in Mexico. "This is an opportunity for Staples to get in on the ground floor with these people and develop relationships that will turn into massively valuable channels for sales and revenue."

Brett couldn't tell if Jay believed what he was saying. Jay's tone gave the impression that he was thinking: *Okay, kid, your dad's a nice guy. But are you sure you can play in this league, or are you just talking a good game?*

The price of admission was small enough to find out. *What's $15,000 or $20,000 to a brand like Staples,* Brett thought, *when it could be in a position to gain fifteen or twenty key accounts?*

"Just being around these young people," Brett pressed, "is a huge opportunity."

"Okay, I'll do it," Jay said. "But all I can give you is $30,000."

Thirty thousand? Brett held his breath. *Did I really just hear that?*

"Jay, if you cut me a check for $30,000," Brett said, "we'll name this entire event after your company!"

And that is how the event in Mexico came to be called the Staples Young Leaders Summit.

As it turns out, that sponsorship would be instrumental in getting the fledgling company through a particularly tough time. By October 2008, only a month before the event in Mexico, the Great Recession had shredded the housing market and cratered stocks. In September, Lehman Brothers, a pillar of the financial community for 158 years and the fourth-largest investment bank in the United States, had filed for bankruptcy. There were deep concerns that the Big Three auto companies would be taken down, along with the city of Detroit. Layoffs immediately began through every region of the country, affecting nearly eight million jobs.

The recession would have given Elliott, Ryan, and Brett every excuse in the world to pull the plug on the second Summit Series event.

But, as we'd soon learn, it's times like these when we need community the most.

6

KNOW YOUR DEFINITION OF SUCCESS

A few months later, Elliott strolled around the hotel grounds at Playa del Carmen with Ryan and Brett, admiring the swimming pool, thatched huts, and quaint cabanas cascading down to a pristine white-sand beach. He explored the activities center and learned about the coral reef and nighttime snorkeling with flashlights and stingrays. *Look at this. It's all ours!*

His guests, however, had a very different reaction when they arrived at the hotel.

"Elliott, there seems to be a mistake. I just checked in and somebody else's stuff is in my room."

"Oh don't worry, it's definitely not a mistake. I know exactly who your roommate is and you're going to have the best connection ever."

"But I want my own room."

"Trust me. Your roommate's incredible. That's how it is at summer camp, and that's how it is here!"

There was almost no time for this strategy to backfire. Once all of the guests had arrived under the thatched roof of the indoor-outdoor hotel restaurant, they were greeted by the first speaker: Scott Harrison. As soon as Scott began sharing his life story, the room grew very quiet.

Scott had lived a very conservative upbringing before he became a nightclub promoter cavorting at the height of extravagance. Vodka bottles in blocks of ice. A model for a girlfriend. The shiny watch he purposely checked every so often so that everyone around him would notice. But after ten years, the lifestyle had started to feel hollow, and Scott decided to join a humanitarian organization doing work in Africa called Mercy Ships. They sent doctors and nurses on floating hospitals to care for those who lacked sufficient access to medical care.

Scott was dispatched to Liberia after a bloody civil war. He was traveling with a group of much-needed volunteer doctors; Liberia itself had only one doctor for every fifty thousand people. The volunteers only had the time and resources for fifteen hundred operations, but seven thousand Liberians showed up in need of surgery.

Some of these people had tumors the size of cantaloupes in their throats that prevented them from breathing comfortably. Many wore towels over their faces because villagers thought the visible tumors meant they were cursed and so they threw rocks at them. In many cases, a forty-five-minute surgery could remove the tumors, but many patients would have to wait several months before receiving treatment.

When Scott asked how the tumors had developed, doctors pointed to the water. Many people were drinking from a brown swamp filled with leeches that stuck to the back of their throats. One remedy to remove these leeches was to drink diesel fuel—strong enough to kill the leeches, but not strong enough to kill the person doing the drinking.

Scott discovered that 80 percent of all diseases in the world were caused by unsanitary water. He learned that in parts of Africa, women were walking eight hours a day with pots filled with thirty pounds of water on their heads, just to have safe water for cooking and washing. He discovered that, for $65, a sand filter could make water drinkable. For $5,000, they could dig a freshwater well.

Scott returned to America, invited seven hundred people to a club using his old party promotion tactics, and raised $15,000—enough to build three wells in northern Uganda. Then he told everyone he didn't want presents on his thirty-second birthday; rather, he asked his friends to donate $32 to his new nonprofit, Charity: Water. The response was overwhelming. Scott not only began to bring clean water to places in need, but with his massive Twitter following, he was able to reach a large audience and significantly scale his impact in a short period of time.

Scott's story provoked the highly successful business owners in the room to reconsider their definitions of success. Was it making money? Or was it making a difference? Everybody who heard Scott speak was forced to look within themselves and question how they wanted to live their lives.

The next day, another speaker under the thatched roof continued to shake assumptions about life and business. By this point, most of the attendees had heard the premise behind author Tim Ferriss's bestselling *The 4-Hour Workweek*: If you could free up your time and work remotely in a place where your dollars stretched a long way, your money would automatically be worth much more. While that extra cash was great, the real value was the ability to live as you wished.

Listening to Tim in person started to tear Elliott out of his childhood home and office in Washington, D.C. From that moment on, he knew that he wanted to travel the world. He wanted to explore. He wanted to grow Summit Series remotely. He looked over and saw the same reaction on Brett's face.

Without quite knowing what he was doing, Elliott had created in Mexico what he had been looking for in college. When he had first arrived at the University of Wisconsin, he had loved the camaraderie of walking to morning classes, feeling the momentum of thousands of students moving in the same direction. It was the sort of energy a marching band tapped into as it headed into the stadium before a college football game.

But one day, on his way to class, Elliott turned and realized he was going exactly where everyone else was headed—to the same classes just to compete for the same jobs—and that thousands of students at other universities were doing the same thing. In that moment, Elliott realized he wanted to walk in the opposite direction.

In Mexico, he was surrounded by a community of people who were united by their values yet walking different paths. Scott and Tim were the teachers Elliott was looking for, and their stories were the classes he desired.

The event ended on the third day with a TOMS shoe drop at a neighboring village. TOMS had partnered with a school district that had a hundred kids wearing beat-up, torn footwear. A group of attendees set up stations, sat on milk crates, and measured the kids' feet. Then they'd grab the right sizes and put the new shoes on them. Elliott looked at the faces of these kids receiving their new shoes and knew right then and there that he was not going back to his windowless office in D.C. to sell digital media space.

A seed was planted in his mind when everyone returned to the hotel. Lively conversations ricocheted around as attendees recounted the inspiring afternoon they had just experienced. The shoe drop had shown Elliott that there was more to business than the bottom line. That building a profitable company and giving back could coexist. He heard the same realization in the conversations around him and began to wonder if Summit Series could one day be the bridge that inspired company founders to want to do more good in the world.

There was no time to dwell on this thought as the energetic buzz of conversations among attendees continued through sunset and into a starlit night sky. Bonds were forming across the pool deck as guests told stories of their trials and tribulations, shared advice, and laughed with one another late into the evening. Finally, the dialogue came to an abrupt halt when Elliott shouted out the idea for a night snorkel. He had masks and fins waiting nearby on the beach, and soon attendees were running as fast as they could to dive into the water. As everyone floated under a vibrant full moon, they finally experienced the first quiet moment of the night.

The next morning, as the event came to a close and everybody checked out of the hotel, the goodbyes were filled with encouragement to take Summit Series further.

"I didn't know what to expect, but I've gotta say, I had an amazing time and met some incredible people."

"Let me know when the next one is—I have some friends I'd like to bring."

It was all the encouragement Elliott needed to take the

final leap and go all in on Summit Series. Back home, his dad's company, Bisnow on Business, was going through a transition. They were hiring new employees and establishing a more professional-sounding name: Bisnow Media. Elliott sensed that it was time for him to evolve, too.

He knew that the life he was returning to would not be the same as the one he'd left. Brett knew he wasn't going back to try to sell real estate during a mortgage crisis. And with Summit Series and Bisnow Media taking off, Ryan was ready to leave his day job.

To consider quitting your job in the middle of the global financial crisis would have seemed insane to most people. General Motors was about to go through bankruptcy and there were mass layoffs around the country. The economy was only getting bleaker, and any job seemed better than no job at all.

But Tim Ferriss had been quick to point out that Apple, FedEx, and Microsoft had all launched in a recession when the economic downturn produced discounted infrastructure, a sudden pool of talented freelancers, and bargain prices. There was no time to lose.

"*Someday,*" Tim loved to say, "is a disease that will take your dreams to the grave with you."

This was the moment to think *bigger*.

Elliott, Ryan, and Brett were ready to double down and throw another event twice the size of the Mexico gathering.

But before they could go all in, they were going to need more help.

7

IF YOU WANT TO GO FAST, GO ALONE. IF YOU WANT TO GO FAR, GO TOGETHER

Over time, trust builds through actions and becomes sturdier, like wet concrete curing. But even after someone has proven to be honest or to give good advice, how do you know if they are the right partner for your company?

After the event in Mexico, Elliott was ecstatic about developing a company of easygoing yet purpose-driven people. It was the first time in his life that he was able to assemble a team, and as a way of helping him figure out who would be a good fit, he came up with a strategy that never would have lasted at a major corporation. The method came from the CollegeHumor guys who'd pranked him with that sartorial note in Park City.

It was a nineties throwback MTV video filmed with a cast of about fifty of Ricky and Josh's young employees. Their team jumped up from their work desks, lip-syncing and dancing to the song "Flagpole Sitta" by Harvey Danger—*I'm not sick but I'm not well / and I'm so hot / 'cause I'm in hell*—ultimately falling to the floor en masse. It was a high-energy, overly dramatic pop punk spoof, but most of all, it gave the impression that there was no place CollegeHumor's employees would rather be working than in their office.

"*That's* what I want," Elliott told himself upon watching the video. It became a tool for him to get a reading on anyone who saw it. He wanted to form a company where the work culture was just as important as the work they were doing. If someone loved the video as much as Elliott did, they were in.

Brett was also on the same page about the video—not to mention that he had over-delivered on sponsorship sales for the Mexico event. Brett had also realized that Summit Series gave him the opportunity to recruit friends he'd want to work with and be around all the time.

When Brett told Elliott he knew two people who'd be great additions to the team, Elliott immediately wanted to meet them. He trusted Brett implicitly because Brett had no filter or hidden agenda. On top of that, Brett had developed the ability to read other people through a simple philosophy:

Lead with generosity.

Generosity creates trust.

Trust creates productivity.

Brett's litmus test was to watch and see if someone reciprocated the same level of generosity they had received from him. If so, he knew he could trust them.

This philosophy attracted the right kind of people to Brett, while his experiences in the college party scene allowed him to quickly detect shady characters. A recommendation from Brett meant a golden seal of approval, and Brett told Elliott that he had trusted Jeff Rosenthal from the moment they had met.

Brett was in college at George Washington at the time, and Jeff was less than four miles away at American University. Brett liked to say there are two priorities for college students. One is grades. The other is a social life. As budding entrepreneurs, Brett and Jeff had both figured out ways to make money off the latter.

They were throwing $10 cover-charge parties at clubs in the D.C. area when they met and combined forces to work on one of Brett's events. Brett picked up on how Jeff genuinely cared for others and how that seemed to put him at the center of everybody. Jeff also noticed this trait in Brett.

The two had a phenomenal night, hitting the club's capacity and bringing in a good chunk of money for themselves. Brett was so impressed with the way Jeff operated that he paid him way beyond their agreed-upon percentage in hopes that Jeff would want to partner again in the future.

And he did. Throughout their college years, Jeff brought American University students to Brett's parties on Thursday nights, and Brett directed GW students to Jeff's parties on Tuesday nights.

But their friendship soared beyond weeknight parties. They started to hang out on weekends and became close with each other's families. They shared a similar thirst for life, but they were also different in many ways. Brett was a showman: high-energy, boisterous, clever, and funny. Jeff was more of an artist: laid-back and articulate, once taking a shot at the designer jewelry business. There was plenty of overlap, though, and they both felt the same initial reservations when they first met Elliott—though Jeff's were more pronounced.

"*That's* the guy?" Jeff had asked Brett after his first interaction with Elliott.

"That's the guy," Brett reaffirmed.

Brett vouched for Elliott because he'd realized that the qualities needed for success aren't surface-level. So what if the guy didn't seem to have an off switch? He delivered on what he said he was going to do, and he worked harder than anyone Brett had ever met.

In fact, during one of his first meetings with Elliott, Brett arrived at 8:00 A.M. to find Elliott already wrapping up a session.

"Impressive," Brett said. "Nice to know I'm your *second* meeting of the day."

"Actually," Elliott pointed out, "you're my *third*. I started with a coffee chat at six-thirty."

Brett had seen what he needed to see in Mexico. Elliott had pulled together a gathering unlike anything Brett had ever experienced—and he was the one known for throwing semester-defining parties. He trusted Elliott.

Jeff had faith in Brett, but it was tough to extend it beyond that. Luckily for Elliott, Jeff saw a personal advantage to joining the team—one that allowed him to benefit from his superpower.

Jeff has the aural version of a photographic memory: He can remember things that were said to him in great detail— that is, if he's paying attention. That's because this blessing comes with a catch: ADHD. If Jeff was sitting in a classroom and didn't care about the subject being taught, he couldn't remember *any* of it; if he did care, he could quote the professor word for word months later. Even though he was smart, he struggled in school in subjects that didn't fascinate him. He was a paradox: a solid C student who'd once skipped a grade.

Because he couldn't learn traditionally, Jeff was almost

completely reliant on taking in information through interactions with friends and mentors. His mind could replay the conversations that engaged him, almost verbatim, years later. He recognized that he needed to surround himself with people who could inspire him. And according to Brett, the Summit Series community would be filled with them.

Brett recounted the Mexico event to Jeff, highlighting all the amazing people he had just spent three days with—all the amazing people that Jeff could have an opportunity to talk with and learn from.

"So it sounds like," Jeff asked Brett, "this is a skeleton key to reach out and call all the people I'd love to meet?"

"That's right," Brett assured him.

That was a lot better than his current job and start-up projects, which left him feeling alone and unfulfilled.

Next, Brett turned to Jeremy Schwartz.

Jeremy had been best friends with Brett since high school. He had a free-flowing, low-key, humble nature, and his rapport with Brett was similar to Jeff's. He was also, in his own way, one of the most successful young businesspeople Brett knew.

Some people wouldn't think of a band as a business, but Jeremy, along with his bandmate Spencer Charnas, had turned Ice Nine Kills into a much-loved commodity. They were not only writing music and running a music publishing company but had also built a loyal fan base around America, created a consistent brand that their generation identified with, and worked out how to make a band their full-time gig. What if Jeremy could apply the same lessons he'd learned touring the country to Summit Series?

Jeremy's band was on the road when Brett reached out. He gave Jeremy a rundown of Summit Series's next phase of growth and showed him press from the Mexico event. That piqued Jeremy's interest. In the music industry, it felt as though everyone was trying to claw their way to the top, while at Summit Series, people were connecting, sharing, and collaborating with one another.

They had long joked that one day either Jeremy would join Brett's future company or Brett would sing for Jeremy's band. So in lieu of a traditional job interview, Brett flew down to Tallahassee, Florida, where Jeremy was playing a sold-out show, and they decided to see who would win out. Brett had been practicing the songs for a couple of months, and in the middle of Ice Nine Kills's set, Jeremy pulled him onstage. Brett grabbed the mic and launched into a highly energetic performance, the crowd singing along with every word he belted out. While he definitely didn't embarrass himself, it was clear to both of them that Brett wasn't going to be a front man. Jeremy joining Summit Series seemed to be the more viable option.

Eager to learn more, on the next break from their tour Jeremy drove from his and Spencer's recording studio in Boston to D.C. to stay with Brett. He wanted to give Summit Series a go.

When Jeremy arrived, his hair was falling past his shoulders and his left eyebrow was pierced. Brett looked at him and told him straight up that he couldn't go into their meetings looking like that; he liked the look, but their less-liberal potential investors might not. If Jeremy wanted to join, he was going to have to cut his hair and lose the piercing.

Jeremy felt his stomach clench. He wasn't prepared for this moment. It said: *Your old life is over.* A part of him wanted to say no. Wearing a suit and tie was counter to all the values on which he'd built his punk rock career. But Jeremy was tired of the grind of touring and was ready for something new.

The two went to the barber together. It was a rite of passage. Jeremy sat down in the chair with his hair looking like Jeff Spicoli's in *Fast Times at Ridgemont High*. When he got up—well, his hair was still covering his ears, but hey, it was a clear sign of commitment.

Jeremy's second test was joining Elliott for a meeting with a prominent magazine publisher with the hopes of getting press coverage for their next event. Even though Jeremy and Elliott had never met, Jeremy figured they would have to give the publisher the impression that they had a long-standing relationship.

"Elliott, great to see you," Jeremy said as he walked into the room, patting him on the back affectionately. "How good was that dinner last night?"

"Oh my God, that grilled brick chicken was unbelievable," Elliott fired back, playing right along.

They nailed the ruse—and the meeting. Elliott left the room immediately sold on Jeremy's ability to think on his feet.

"But," he said, "you're gonna have to cut that hair."

"But I just did!"

The team was formed. Everyone was excited to hit the road—all except Ryan.

Ryan had graduated from Northwestern, worked at Deutsche Bank, and landed a job at a top private equity firm. He wanted to be an entrepreneur and part of Summit Series—but he also wanted to run a business from a fixed office with an established home. So Ryan began to straddle two jobs:

running operations for Summit Series and being Bisnow's
CEO, which was expanding from D.C. to New York City, soon
Chicago, and eventually twenty-eight more cities.

This actually ended up working out in everyone's favor.
Elliott gave up his position at Bisnow Media to Ryan. In
doing so, it liberated Elliott to head out into the world with
Brett, Jeff, and Jeremy to grow Summit Series.

There was just one question left: Where would we go?

It was the dead of winter in early 2009, and D.C. was mis-
erably cold. We were fantasizing about sunnier climates
around the world, but at the time we could barely afford to
shell out enough for dinner, let alone four international plane
tickets. Then, in yet another stroke of luck, Brett stumbled
across the perfect alternative.

"I have some great news that's going to change our lives,"
he said. His grandmother was offering us her two-bedroom
condo on a nine-hole golf course in Boca Raton. It was in an
age-restricted community, sure, but as long as we pretended
like we were her guests, everything would be golden. "That
means that the four of us can get out of this cold weather and
have our own home in sunny Florida for the next four months
to do whatever we want."

Never mind that we'd be the youngest people in this community by a good fifty years—it was a chance to downsize,
live cheaply, and pour ourselves into our new business, all
while living poolside. The four of us celebrated, and, with a
final nod to Tim Ferriss, decided to reduce what we owned
down to one carry-on suitcase each. We donated our furniture to Goodwill. There were only a few remaining pieces
in Brett's D.C. apartment when he ceremoniously karate-
chopped through a flimsy desk. The chop felt like breaking

through an old way of life. Bye-bye, desk. Bye-bye, office. Bye-bye, city.

We were four guys in our early twenties with no big-business experience, no savings, and no fear. The recession might have demolished our chances of stable, traditional careers—not that we would have been satisfied with day jobs anyway—but it also gave us the chance to create a new kind of community out of the rubble. This kind of naive bravado is the type of lucid insanity many start-ups need to get themselves off the ground—to deny the sensible option and choose the most outlandish one instead.

And quite often, with that kind of a giant leap, you're ripe to make a big mistake.

8

REPUTATIONS ARE EARNED BY THE DROP AND LOST BY THE BUCKET

It felt like we were gaming the system. We were supposed to have jobs, but instead we were building a company while sitting poolside in the subtropical Florida air. Granted, it was a pool at a retirement community, and the four of us had to share two beds. But we had our own house, it was sunny, and we had a body of water to jump into as we planned our future.

The community we moved into felt like a scene out of *Pleasantville*. We were surrounded by perfectly manicured lawns, gnomes in front gardens, and quilts on porches. There was a hushed silence by the pool while octogenarians played backgammon—a serenity we broke when we began making phone calls.

We wanted the next Summit Series event to show a level of sophistication that we definitely didn't embody. So we pushed ourselves to elevate the experience.

We landed on a ski weekend in Aspen at the stately St. Regis. The luxury hotel is part of a renowned chain spanning the globe that was started in New York back in 1904 by John Jacob Astor IV, one of the wealthiest men on the planet at the time. At the Aspen St. Regis, the bathrooms were all marble. The linens had a thread count of four hundred. They used a saber to open bottles of champagne. There was even butler service.

No more summer camp. That vibe may have worked at our past two events, but we felt it was time to step it up.

Truthfully, we didn't even have the money to *go* to Aspen to check it out. So we booked the hotel's ballroom and some restaurants in town, sight unseen, from our poolside cabana. We didn't gut-check any of this with our former attendees— we were excited, so we figured they would be, too.

The problem was, there was simply no way we could continue to offer a free event, especially with the global economy plummeting. Based on the crowd we'd pulled for the last two events, we got *GQ* to put up a little money to co-host Aspen, but because we were now in the middle of a recession, there were very few sponsors willing to chip in. We were on the hook for hundreds of thousands of dollars and could no longer cover losses of that scale with credit cards.

For any business, there's a critical point when founders must decide to monetize their company. Many organizations establish a revenue model right out of the gate and start charging for its product from day one. The downside of this strategy is the risk of turning away your customers before they've even had a chance to experience what you're offering. Another effective strategy is based on the concept of "try before you buy." It's why the "freemium" model works so well for many digital products. It's why Costco doles out free samples of pizza rolls in front of the frozen food section. Summit Series was no different. We had given people a taste of what we were offering, and they had liked it. So we figured we could now start charging people to attend, and establish our revenue model based on ticket sales.

We figured that most of our audience could afford a $3,000 ticket. After all, they were some of the most successful young business leaders in America. They'd gotten great value from the earlier events, and they trusted us to deliver on our promises. We assumed they'd find the value of the relationships they'd forge well worth the ticket price.

What we didn't realize was that it's hard for people to be critical of your product when they're getting it for free. Elliott had received nothing but hugs and high fives at the close of the first event in Utah. Brett had heard only praise in Mexico. And Jeff and Jeremy knew only what they'd been told— that nearly every attendee was thrilled with their experience.

Because we assumed that everyone loved what we did, we didn't feel like we had to seek out advice or get feedback from past attendees on if they would be willing to pay to attend. We decided to push forward without consulting anyone.

Elliott drafted an email with complete confidence that we'd sell out in a few days. He sat by the pool, shirtless, tapping away on his laptop. "All right, are you guys ready to watch hundreds of thousands of dollars flow into our bank account as soon as I hit send?"

He glanced at his email one last time and smiled.

We'll have 125 of the most influential people in America under 35 years old.

We are not releasing a list of people who are booking or have booked due to the high profile of attendees on the trip.

Elliott liked an invitation he'd seen to a party in Washington that came with three rules as an homage to *Fight Club,* and he'd lifted the format. It was the perfect formula to bury the fact that attendees would have to pay for their own tickets.

There are 3 rules for Aspen 09:

1. Don't tell anyone about Aspen 09.

2. There are no comped tickets.

3. Don't tell anyone about Aspen 09.

"See ya in Aspen!" the last line read, along with a link to the website where attendees could purchase their ticket for $3,000.

Elliott looked up. "Ready, gentlemen? Here's to a bold future!"

Then he hit send on his computer and let it fly.

Elliott's enthusiasm was contagious, and the four of us, feeling satisfied with ourselves, decided to celebrate by hitting the golf course for the afternoon. But before we could even pack up from the pool, we got our first call. We picked up the phone fully expecting it to be an excited invitee ready with their credit card details.

We couldn't have been more wrong. The person on the other end of the phone was so upset about our terrible communication that he felt compelled to call us rather than type an email.

"This is offensive. You traded on our names for your own profit."

We thought that maybe this was just one outlier, a single disappointed customer in a sea of happy campers. But then the emails started rolling in.

"You should really evaluate how you do business."

"Thanks, but no thanks. I'm definitely *not* coming."

And those were just from the folks who felt compelled to tell us how badly we'd screwed up. Many didn't bother to respond at all.

Maybe they hated the smug tone. Maybe they hated our *Fight Club* reference. Maybe they felt we sounded entitled or tone-deaf. We quickly realized they mostly hated that we'd sprung such a big change on them without explaining why. The last two Summit Series events had been free, and here we were demanding that everybody pay $3,000 for the privilege of continuing to attend.

Some people in the community saw the email for what it was—a novice mistake. But perhaps our most egregious offense was making people who cared about us feel like they were the victims of a bait-and-switch after they'd turned over the personal contacts of their closest friends.

As waves of guilt and anxiety crashed down upon us, we scrambled to send a follow-up email to try to smooth things over, explaining why we could no longer sustain Summit Series events without charging. But it was too late.

The situation only deteriorated. One of the recipients leaked our email to Gawker, which put us on the front page of their website under the headline "The $3,000 Invite for Startup Founders' Ski-Bum Party."

We moved through our own stages of grief: from disbelief to panic, and then to anger, devastation, and finally acceptance.

We decided to push forward, but after many days, we'd sold only ten tickets—which was miraculous in its own right—and we were running out of time to cancel our contract with the St. Regis. Our fear that we had lost our community's trust was now turning into financial fear, too.

Ryan called in from D.C., pragmatic but not pleased. "Look," he said, "we're going to take a bath on this thing. We should exercise our attrition clause with the St. Regis to reduce our exposure."

He took it even further, suggesting we consider the possibility that the business model might not be viable. Offering a free party was one thing. Selling $3,000 tickets to an event was entirely different. He recommended a sensible retreat for all of us back to Bisnow Media.

"My sister in Westchester County just got a black Labrador and they have extra puppies," he said. "If we exercise our attrition clause, we'll all have money to get some dogs."

None of us in Florida were ready to concede. But we had to consider Ryan's view. Our community (if you could even call it that at this point) was upset. They felt betrayed. They felt we had pulled a fast one on them. Maybe this just wasn't going to work.

Elliott felt so guilty about the email that he seriously considered shutting everything down. If he'd been the only founder, there's a good chance he would have. But that was the beauty of partnership.

Brett looked over at Jeff and Jeremy. He'd recruited them. He'd asked Jeremy to ditch his aspirations as a musician and join the team. And what was Jeff supposed to do now, go back to Macy's? And where was Brett going to find real estate work in the deepening recession?

The more Brett thought about it, the more adamant he became. *This is what I've wanted. I've wanted to make it on my own, not spend my days working for a corporate entity. I put myself on the line to recruit the people who I wanted to spend my time around. We're all in this together now. This is what I want to fight for.*

"Fold this epic business idea with so much potential just so we can go get some puppies?" he asked. "No way."

Brett was under no delusions. He knew the main tree of attendees, which had grown so quickly, was almost dead. But he believed that if we carefully nurtured three or four seedlings, we could begin to regrow a forest.

He proposed employing a tactic that came from a sensible, proven place: the "family and friends" approach of selling Cutco knives. While he had no plans to sell cutlery to Summit Series attendees, this basic sales principle was Brett's source of confidence. Start with the people in your circle and spiral out from there through referrals. It had worked in his knife-selling and nightclub-promoting days. If you grow your audience organically through the people you already know, you can build meaningful relationships that will do your networking *for* you.

Ten people had bought tickets to the Aspen event. *They* were happy. Brett suggested we reach out to those ten, pick up referrals, and rebuild from there. We needed to sell more than a hundred spots in less than two months, and during a recession, no less. But there were now four of us on board to build new relationships.

We had a huge hole to climb out of, and it was risky, but there really was no alternative. We had to believe it was possible.

And then we got lucky when things took an unexpected turn. We learned that the White House had a dilemma.

9

OPPORTUNITIES CAN COME FROM ANYWHERE

Our luck started when Elliott decided that it was important to try to pay down some of the debt he and Ryan
had accrued from the first two events. He may not have been
good at sending subtle emails, but he had a knack for selling
newsletter ads. So in late February 2009—not long after
President Obama's first inauguration—Elliott returned to
Washington, D.C., for a meeting to try to make a deal on the
side for Bisnow Media. The meeting had been set up over a
tennis game, and Elliott had just finished playing when his
phone rang.

We all believed that opportunities could come from
anywhere—a neighbor, a friend, a mentor—and you never
knew where an introduction or conversation might lead, so
always take the meeting or pick up the phone when it rings.
This opportunity happened to come from Elliott's mother,
Margot. She was calling from a friend's party. She had been
introduced to a man who worked in politics and thought
Elliott might want to meet him.

"What's his name?" Elliott inquired.

"Yosi Sergant."

"Yosi Sergant?"

Yosi had become famous for being the driving force behind the iconic Shepard Fairey "Hope" poster that symbolized Barack Obama's 2008 presidential campaign—and victory.

This is a huge opportunity, Elliott thought. Much bigger than whatever advertising deal he was chasing. He quickly excused himself, raced home to change clothes, then zoomed off to the party at a Georgetown townhouse, hoping that Yosi would still be there.

Call it luck, call it a happy coincidence, but Elliott knew if he didn't pounce on this opportunity, nothing would come of it. He walked in and immediately relaxed when he saw Yosi was still there.

He introduced himself—as Casino-Floor-Elliott liked to do—and they spoke for nearly half an hour. Elliott learned that Yosi led outreach for what President Obama had renamed the Office of Public Engagement. Yosi had been tasked with hosting one of the first important business-related events for the new White House administration. It was a symposium for roughly forty influential CEOs under forty years old to discuss the issues that entrepreneurs and tech businesses faced in the economic crisis.

The timing was particularly important. Throughout the transition, news was swirling about the economy getting worse by the day. There had been tremendous blowback after big auto leaders, whose companies were seeking government bailouts, flew to D.C. to speak to Congress—on their companies' private jets. The focus on the big companies and the mismanagement of finances had left many small-business owners feeling slighted. The administration saw a meeting with young entrepreneurs as a burst of positive energy.

Elliott recognized that Yosi was essentially trying to host a Summit Series event at the White House. The administration needed to make a connection with America's most promising young business leaders so that it could establish relationships, explain the current economic situation, and, ultimately, get insight on issues that affected the next generation.

But Yosi had a problem, because the Office of Public Engagement had no budget for this symposium, nothing planned, and no confirmed attendees. And there was one other slight issue: The event was due to take place in a week.

Elliott saw his chance, and he took it.

"I've been working to connect that same community," Elliott told Yosi. "I just had an event for sixty company founders in Mexico." He began sharing the stories of the Summit Series attendees, glossing over the fact that many of them were currently furious with him.

"What if we set it up for you?" Elliott concluded.

It was a huge risk—both for the White House and for the four of us.

Yosi had no assurance that we could pull off his event. And Elliott knew we needed every minute to right our own ship and try to sell tickets to Aspen. Besides, we weren't an event-for-hire company—and there wasn't even any payment offered. On top of that, we had no idea if we'd have ties to the forty people the White House wanted to invite. This potentially meant making cold calls to the kinds of people whose schedules are booked down to the minute for months in advance.

"I'll need to work out some details on my end," Yosi said, "but I'll circle back with you in a few days."

Elliott's brain whirled on his return flight to Florida. Sometimes you can push and push and get nowhere. Sometimes a better solution to a problem is to step out of the mud you're in and think bigger. A quantum leap sure beats crawling inch by inch, and the White House—and all the doors it might open—was a very long way from that retirement condo.

When Elliott arrived back at the condo, he was very upbeat. "You'll never guess what just happened in D.C.," he said. "I met this guy named Yosi Sergant. He's working for the White House. He might do an event with us."

The three of us wanted to believe him, but we were a little hesitant. The White House? Really?

"Really," Elliott said. "Yosi may call."

Every time Elliott's phone rang for the next four days, someone shouted, "Is that Yosi?"

Time after time we teased Elliott whenever he leapt for his phone—that is, until a call lit up his mobile on a Friday night, and Elliott looked at the screen and said, "Yes!"

The three of us rushed over to gather around him as he put Yosi on speaker.

"All right," Yosi said, "I got you the event. We're confirmed for next Friday morning. It'll be for two hours. I'm sending over the list of the guests we'd like in attendance. Oh, and I'll need all their social security numbers and dates of birth by Tuesday, HOP."

"HOP?" Elliott asked.

"Head on pillow. By Tuesday night, before you fall asleep, I need those numbers. And bring the founders of Method. They're doing great things. Good luck!" The phone clicked.

The four of us looked at each other in weighted silence. We had four days to get forty of the country's top entrepreneurs to come to D.C. on the following Friday.

That moment was when we truly realized we were a team—a bunch of partners who were willing to take a crazy risk. If we had to convince each other that this was doable, we wouldn't have had time to pull it off. The three of us responded to the situation as instinctively as Elliott had the moment he'd met Yosi.

Jeff was the first to break the silence. "I'll work on getting Ev Williams from Twitter."

Jeremy chimed in, "I'll work on the branding materials so this thing actually feels legitimate. And I guess I'll figure out a way to securely store everyone's social security numbers."

Brett was already Googling the number for the Method founders. "I'll make the call," he said.

Yosi's problem was our gift. We now had the ultimate reason to reach out to some of the busiest, hardest-to-reach people on the planet with a pitch that sounded almost too good to be true. And we got to use the magic word of the moment: Obama.

We didn't know how we were going to pull it off, but we immediately turned Brett's grandma's condo into a boiler room and began to work our way down the forty-person list. We started with the two people the White House had specifically requested, Adam Lowry and Eric Ryan from Method cleaning products.

Brett channeled his best knife-salesperson days, reached for his BlackBerry, and dialed.

"Hello, my name is Brett Leve and I'm calling from Summit Series. We're hosting an event at the White House next Friday and the administration specifically requested that Adam and Eric join. It's going to discuss economic policy, and they want to hear from young entrepreneurs. Would Adam and Eric be able to attend?"

The person on the other end of the line said they were very flattered to hear that, but unfortunately Adam and Eric would not be available. They were giving a talk in San Diego on that day.

"Would it be possible for them to cancel and come to D.C. instead?"

There was a pause at the other end of the line.

"*Excuse me?*"

"We really think Adam and Eric should attend this event. It's much more important."

"Sir, you're asking me to tell my boss to cancel a paid speaking engagement with less than a week's notice to go to something called Summit Series? I've never even heard of that."

Brett was losing the battle. He decided to change tactics.

"It's not Summit Series that's requesting Adam and Eric's presence here—it's the president of the United States of America, Barack Obama. Your bosses have built a wonderful business in this country, and now their country needs them."

Brett took the longest power pause of his life. Then he went on, his words slow and drawn out: "There's no other way to say this. But when the White House calls, *you answer.*"

Well, that sure sounded a lot better than: "When Brett Leve from Boca Raton calls, *you answer.*"

Thankfully, it worked. We had our first two attendees.

We began the barrage of phone calls, adding the confirmed attendees' names to the pitches as we went. We learned that it's okay to call somebody late on a Saturday night if you have exciting news for them. There's no bad time to bring someone a great opportunity. Nearly half of the attendees, we later found out, had suspicions about the event.

But they said yes despite their skepticism because they wanted to buy what we were selling as much as we wanted to sell it.

As we went through the list of CEOs, real estate moguls, and tech entrepreneurs, we'd listen in on each other's calls to learn what parts of our script were working and what parts weren't. We realized we were nobodies in the eyes of these luminaries, so we needed to come up with a compelling argument for them to want to take our calls.

Then one evening, as we were casually perusing YouTube, we came across a Nike commercial titled "Take It to the Next Level." It was a fast-paced video from a first-person perspective of an up-and-coming soccer player, featuring well-known athletes. In that moment, we realized the power of brand co-opting. Nike leveraged the aspirational nature of elite athletes to position its brand as a leader in the space. It dawned on us that we had one of the most prestigious brands at our fingertips: the White House. What if we ran the same playbook?

So we came up with a killer opening line. When the person on the other end of the phone picked up, we'd wait for a few seconds until the silence was palpable, and then we'd say: "Good afternoon. This is Elliott Bisnow calling with an invitation from the White House."

As preposterous as it was, we actually were calling on behalf of the White House, which instantly sparked a conversation and positioned each of us as someone worth taking the time to speak with.

While the rest of us were using our seasoned sales experience on those calls, Jeremy was cementing his value to the group in other ways. He could command a stage in front of thousands of people, but without any sales experience, he was less comfortable extending that same casual confidence to pitching strangers. So he began taking on all the overlooked but crucial tasks that hadn't crossed anyone else's mind. Jeremy had found his place among us without even a word of discussion—and with four days to pull off a miracle, there was no time to waste.

Back when Jeremy was in a band, he understood that making music was only one piece of the puzzle. What was the point of writing songs if no one knew about them? He'd seen the importance of building up an online presence through social media and websites, so he'd taught himself to code. He'd soon realized the importance of a band's image—from logo design to marketing campaigns—so he'd taught himself Photoshop and taken a course on graphic design. By the time he joined Summit Series, Jeremy was by no means a marketing or tech expert, but he had developed his skills enough to dive right in.

With less than ninety-six hours to go, this was exactly what we needed. While Jeff, Brett, and Elliott hit the phones for twenty-one hours a day, Jeremy managed everything else: building a secure system to store the attendees' social security numbers, creating the look and feel of the entire event, coordinating the logistics, and designing everything from program guides to lanyards.

When it came time to put the finishing touches on the cover of the program guide, he placed an image of the White House logo next to the Summit Series logo, stamped it with the presidential seal so the guide looked official, and sent it off for printing. And just like that, we looked like a legitimate organization, when in reality we were barely keeping it all together.

Ninety-six hours after Yosi's call, we had secured the attendance of thirty-five of some of the most prominent young entrepreneurs in America.

But as stressful as getting those yeses was, it was only the first step. We had been given a golden chance to impress these incredibly high-profile people, but now we had to pull off what we were promising. This wasn't the same as failing to buy enough beer for a bunch of start-up founders in Utah. If we failed this time, there was a much greater—and more public—height to fall from. We wouldn't just be disappointing our attendees and ourselves. We'd be disappointing the new administration.

As scary as it was, the White House had called. And we were sure as hell going to answer.

10

MYSTERY MAKES HISTORY

We had the yeses. We had confirmed everyone's travel plans and accommodations. We had organized security clearances. As it turned out, that was the easy part. Now, we needed to transport attendees to another place—a *surreal* place.

Our biggest fear was that everyone would show up and the event would go fine. But one thing we've learned about events is that *fine* is worse than no event at all. You've put your credibility on the line. You've told everyone it's going to be amazing. And afterward, if everyone is left thinking, "That was *it?*," you've failed.

We wanted to build a business around delivering something better than expected; over-promise, then over-deliver. So we turned our attention toward making the day momentous.

The White House was handling the two-hour symposium—the actual policy work—but we wanted to turn the whole day into an experience. We had no idea what tangible results would come out of the symposium, but we knew that if the event was just a two-hour one-and-done, it would be a disappointment. So we began building other plans around it, from breakfast through nightcaps, to make the entire experience unforgettable and filled with meaning.

It's great to go to the White House and get a briefing. You feel important, you feel wanted. But do you feel listened to? Do you feel that you've formed connections? Aside from the economic input, we knew that any real changes that might come out of that briefing wouldn't be apparent until much later. We had an opportunity to facilitate new collaborations among business leaders. Collaborations that had the potential to boost economic recovery and create new opportunities during the worst economic collapse in almost a century.

Well, we weren't just going to sit back and watch. We weren't going to be afraid to get involved and try to take this symposium from a level ten to an eleven, even if no one asked us to. We figured the more people who were talking about this event, the more important it would feel to everyone attending. We weren't going to lose this opportunity.

We needed to create a buzz. Because the event was private, there was no public press release. But what was the point of these entrepreneurs encouraging the White House to support small business if no one knew about it? We wanted them to be taken seriously.

We knew *The Washington Post* wouldn't listen to some kids in their early twenties. We had barely received any press to date, and the limited press we *had* received wasn't exactly flattering. But we'd heard about something called "whisper campaigns." We live in a noisy world. Sometimes if you want to be heard, the solution is to proceed a little more quietly in order to pique curiosity.

We happened to be in just the right place to make this strategy work. Elliott had grown up in D.C., and Brett and Jeff had gone to college there. Plus, after Jeff left American University's soccer team, he'd taken a job as likely the youngest professional floor staff member in the history of Congress. We figured we could reach out to the few friends we had made in Washington to generate excitement.

We told everyone we knew in D.C. that something big was going down. When they asked what it was, we vaguely told them it was a meeting happening on government grounds, but that we couldn't say more. We called the Treasury Department's executive offices: "Is Secretary Geithner aware of the meeting this Friday?"

Elliott called Ryan asking, "Know anyone at the White House?"

"Yeah, I know someone," Ryan replied.

"Really? Who?" asked Elliott.

"Well, I mean, I know someone who I think knows someone," Ryan said, smirking.

Ryan made a few calls and found his way to the cellphone of Jason Furman, a top economic advisor for Obama. He asked Jason if he'd be attending the gathering. Jason hadn't heard of it, but the seed was planted. Jason asked around his office inquiring about the meeting. Soon the staff inside the White House were asking each other about what this influential gathering was about and who else from the White House should attend.

It was now early March 2009. The new administration was still being assembled. Nobody wanted to feel left out, especially as the hierarchy was beginning to gel. Officials started asking for invitations. We heard that when Rahm Emanuel, Obama's chief of staff, spoke to Yosi, he demanded to know why he hadn't been invited. Minutes later, Yosi was on the phone with Elliott, wanting to know how Emanuel could possibly have heard about such an under-the-radar event. Then when Evan Williams, the CEO of Twitter, tweeted about the event the day before, everything exploded.

The controversy might have led to the event being canceled if Yosi hadn't stepped in to calm everyone's nerves and push the meeting forward. Maybe we overshot the landing just a bit—but it worked. It worked because we got *involved*. Members of the team putting together the stimulus package soon confirmed to attend the symposium. So did the people advising President Obama on economic policy, along with those involved with social media and environmental initiatives. Everyone got more engaged.

That never would've happened if we'd hired a public relations firm to put out a press release. Spreading our own story got us way more press than any traditional PR could.

In that moment, we learned a very important storytelling strategy, which we use at Summit Series to this day: "Mystery makes history."

11

CULTURE STEAMROLLS STRATEGY

We woke before sunrise on event day in Elliott's parents' house in D.C. This was it.

A few hours later, the event began. Everyone was seated for breakfast in the Lafayette Room of the Hay-Adams Hotel, which is apparently *the* place to stay in D.C. President Obama had even lived at the hotel with his family before the inauguration. We were served in old-school D.C. style: starched white tablecloth, glistening china, waiters with napkins draped over their arms. We imagined it was the same as when Charles Lindbergh or Amelia Earhart visited in the thirties.

The Lafayette Room hummed with power. We asked all the attendees to introduce themselves.

"I'm Rob Speyer of Tishman Speyer, and I just flew in from India to be here."

"Hi, I'm Tony Hsieh, CEO of Zappos."

"I'm Evan Williams from Twitter."

"Hi, I'm Jessica Jackley and I co-founded Kiva, and I'm so glad to be part of this group."

The co-founder of Twitter was sitting next to the head of one of the world's largest microfinance organizations. The founders of Method were having breakfast next to Catherine Levene of DailyCandy.

The four of us knew that we had no business being in the room. While these folks were building businesses that provided a backbone for America's struggling economy, Jeff had been planning fashion lines for Macy's and Jeremy had been subsisting off roadside hamburgers while touring with his punk band.

After everyone finished breakfast, we took a quick walk across Lafayette Park to the Eisenhower Executive Office Building for the briefing on economic policy.

The White House knew that these two hours wouldn't immediately solve the economic crisis. But it genuinely wanted to get to know the people attending, and it hoped that those two hours would yield forty incredible introductions. The White House would soon have a personal relationship with Twitter, which was only beginning to show its potential as a powerful promotion tool. Angel investor Chris Sacca could introduce his growing portfolio of start-up companies to help the administration solve a variety of problems. Over the next eight years, the White House would collaborate with many people in that room.

But not every important conversation occurred in the conference room. During the symposium, Jeff noticed that some of the attendees were leaving the room to talk with each other in the corridor instead. The insight coming from the government was fascinating—but sometimes you learn more by conversing than by being lectured. As the ancient proverb states, "Tell me and I forget. Teach me and I remember. *Involve* me and I learn." That was exactly how Jeff learned. After seeing some of the most powerful moments happen offstage, Jeff made certain that the concept of the corridor was a large part of our future events. We wanted to provide an intimate space where people could reflect and discuss on the sidelines.

After the symposium, we headed back to the Hay-Adams for some roundtable discussions where attendees got to know each other better. As organizers, we remained at a respectful distance. The conversations were so far over our heads that we wouldn't have dared to try to get a word in, anyway. But we could see how energized everyone was by dinnertime.

The White House was Jeff's first Summit Series event, and he could tell how the simple act of breaking bread brought people together. It wasn't the polished silverware or extravagant ambiance that elicited connection. It was the energy that blossomed from eye contact, body language, tone of voice, and conversation. This was Jeremy's first event, too, and he was stunned at how deeply attendees were bonding over the dinner table. *You couldn't separate them if you tried,* he thought.

None of this was lost on Yosi. He pulled us aside and said, "What you're doing is important. You guys have a superpower: the ability to convene. Use this power for good. I'm not talking about just throwing parties. I'm talking about convening people to make an impact on the world."

We thought about the email we'd sent announcing the Aspen event and how it had taught us that *not* asking for feedback can destroy your business. Now we were paying attention and receptive to any advice we could get, especially from someone like Yosi. That's when we were hit with an unexpected bolt of wisdom.

Tony Hsieh from Zappos came over to us and asked us a simple question: "Are there people at this event who you wouldn't invite to your parents' home for dinner, if not for their personal and professional success?"

Yes, we admitted, there were some. Although professionally accomplished, not everyone in the room shared our values. We had worked off a list the White House supplied that reflected the administration's values, and then added a handful of our own contacts.

"Those people can't be part of what you're building going forward," Tony told us. "If you're building a community, your culture is the most important thing."

He'd go on to write a book called *Delivering Happiness,* and he understood the concept of creating a community through culture at the highest level. Tragically, Tony passed away in 2020. But the impact he left on our organization will reverberate for our lifetime. The wisdom he imparted to us that night changed the trajectory of Summit Series.

The afterparty ended at 2 A.M. The four of us stayed up until sunrise talking over what we'd just experienced. We weren't high-fiving ourselves; we were trying to identify what had worked, what hadn't, and where to take Summit Series next. Thanks to Tony, we stopped thinking of our company as a series of ongoing independent events and began to explore the idea of it being a means of building an ongoing, lasting community. Moving forward, the composition of our attendees would boil down to two simple questions:

1. Do the people we want to invite do innovative work in the world?
2. Are they kind, open-minded people with a true desire to grow?

Those criteria may seem simple, almost obvious—but they're very powerful. Those two questions changed the course of Summit Series dramatically. Until that night, we lacked the language to describe what we wanted to build. We were moving from event to event, but not thinking of Summit Series in the larger sense of a *community*.

An idea is not fully formed until it's articulated in just the right words. The kinds of highly sophisticated people we wanted as attendees were hard to get hold of, so when we did, it was important that we be able to define Summit Series in a clear, concise, inspiring way. When you can explain your mission clearly, you give other people—and yourself—something to believe in.

The wording in our newly crafted attendee criteria also conveyed that there was no financial benchmark. We wouldn't limit our events to Fortune 500 executives. This opened us up to a wider spectrum of talent, including artists, nonprofit leaders, scientists, and chefs—to name a few—who could all contribute to and enhance the fabric of our community. We wanted to make it clear that everybody who shared our passion was included, not just people on "25 Under 25" lists.

When we reflected back on the Aspen event, we realized it was the *wording* of that poorly crafted email that had gotten us into trouble, not the concept. Instead of being transparent, we'd hidden behind humor. Instead of being vulnerable, we'd been cocky. Instead of thinking about others, we'd been thinking about ourselves. Now we knew how to tell our story. We could explain that we were building a community of innovators across industries and disciplines, who were also kind and open-minded—people we'd want to be friends with regardless of professional success.

Who wouldn't want to join that?

When we woke up the morning after the White House event, it felt like we were no longer trudging through the mud, struggling to make the Aspen event anything but a failure. We now knew exactly how to move forward, and we were ready to go.

The White House event not only gave us a second chance, it gave us a backstory. Before the event, when people asked us about our past, what could we say about ourselves? That we were ordering more fast fashion for Macy's, or selling ads for our dad's online newsletter?

Yes, we had thrown a couple of parties for entrepreneurs. But the White House event brought a new level of gravitas we had never experienced before. We now had something to talk about. We also had a lot of new friends who could connect us to people making an impact.

But we had to turn this renewed motivation and fresh opportunity into reality. With our Aspen event fast approaching and ticket sales trickling in slowly, we were going to need all the new friends we could find—and fast.

12

A SINGLE CONNECTION CAN BE EXPONENTIAL

We used the excitement of the White House gathering to push ahead with our Aspen event, knowing full well that if we didn't fill the hotel rooms we'd booked at the St. Regis, we were going to be in a deep financial hole.

We thought we had rescued ourselves after lining up what looked like a high-priced sponsorship with Raymond Weil watches. The company initially said it was going to put up $100,000. But over time, that number kept shrinking. Soon it was $20,000. Then it was $7,000. Then it was $2,000 and four watches.

It was tough to feel this squeeze while trying to remain grateful to one of our few sponsors, but we had no choice. We needed every dollar we could get.

We accepted that we'd lost a large percentage of our original attendees due to the email fiasco, so we implemented Brett's friends-and-family strategy, asking our booked attendees to introduce us to people in their network. It worked. Ticket sales picked up slowly, and we inched our way toward our goal. Many business opportunities, we learned, will bubble to the surface with a bit of luck and persistence. You send email after email, make phone call after phone call—and then you get that one crucial introduction. All it takes is one person to change everything.

For us, that person was a vibrant, fun-loving Texan who rescued the Aspen event, setting off a series of connections that changed Summit Series forever.

Her name: Elizabeth Gore.

When we first met Elizabeth, she was the head of global partnerships for the United Nations Foundation, a nonprofit that works alongside the UN for support. It was started by Ted Turner, founder of CNN, after Ted felt embarrassed that the United States refused to meet its global dues to the UN. Ted donated $1 billion of his own money to the foundation to back his belief that the world should solve its problems together.

We quickly formed a deep friendship with Elizabeth as we discovered a shared passion. When we recounted the shoe drop experience from our Mexico event and how it inspired us to connect entrepreneurs with organizations doing good in the world, she saw that we wanted to use our platform for good, and she felt the UN Foundation could help.

She took us under her wing. Being around Elizabeth made it clear that we needed to create a more inclusive community. We realized how much we were lacking by not integrating different perspectives.

"You need female speakers?" Elizabeth asked. "How about Ellen Gustafson and Lauren Bush, the co-founders of FEED? Their nonprofit has provided more than a hundred million meals for those in need around the world through the sale of tote bags."

An introduction from Elizabeth made for a very easy phone call. Ellen and Lauren were all in to speak at our Aspen event. Elizabeth also helped us realize that we could make a financial contribution on behalf of Summit Series to the issues that mattered most to us in the form of an auction. "How about dinner with Ted Turner?" Elizabeth asked. We'd never thrown an auction before, but we were excited to see what kind of funding we could generate. We were all in.

It's impossible to calculate the value of Elizabeth's mentorship. After months of struggling to attract sponsors, our new association with the UN Foundation helped legitimize our work. Elizabeth trusted us with her brand, even though she knew we had little experience. She trusted us to do right by the women she introduced us to.

We were truly overwhelmed by her generosity, but what we hadn't realized was that Summit Series had helped her in a way, too. Elizabeth often felt like her job at the foundation was like pushing a boulder up a hill. The UN is highly bureaucratic and not accustomed to solving problems in entrepreneurial ways. It worked with governments and heads of state at a steady, plodding pace. Entrepreneurs, on the other hand, approached problems as though they were jumping out of a plane without a parachute and figuring out how to sew one on the way down. Trying to merge those two styles of business seemed impossible.

But Elizabeth was trying. And we could connect her with those parachute-less young risk-takers.

One of Elizabeth's most innovative ideas was to collaborate with the NBA to fight malaria through a program called Nothing but Nets. Malaria is not often spoken about in the United States, but it's a huge problem around the world, especially in sub-Saharan Africa. Every two minutes a child dies of the disease. Bed nets injected with insecticide are a simple, cost-effective way to prevent malaria, and Elizabeth was using basketball stars to help promote the bed nets. A well-known sports columnist wrote a magazine story asking for $10 donations. This was a solid launch, but the campaign needed a booster rocket.

Elizabeth told us we could save a lot of lives if the auction proceeds went to Nothing but Nets. She also suggested we invite the humanitarian who designed the nets the organization was distributing: Mikkel Vestergaard Frandsen.

Hardly any of the 120 people who bought tickets to the Aspen event knew of Elizabeth Gore or Mikkel Vestergaard Frandsen. Most of our attendees were founders of tech start-ups. But as it turned out, this collision between technology and social justice was just what we needed, and it would teach us a big lesson: The best connections are exponential.

Everything Elizabeth taught us back then led to everything we became. Without her introductions, Mikkel, or the auction, we would've been left with an ordinary ski trip. We knew Summit Series could be so much more than that. Now we just had to prove it to everyone else.

13

WHEN YOU KNOW HOW TO LISTEN, EVERYBODY IS A GURU

We wish we could say that the Aspen event went smoothly. That we managed to flawlessly pull off the programming we'd planned on that snowy April weekend in 2009.

But that's just not how it went down. Though the surroundings were luxurious, they didn't suit the sensibilities of our attendees. Many of them were young company founders in tech who made money sitting behind a computer screen coding. Some had never been to a hotel like the St. Regis before—one that greeted them with complimentary bathrobes and slippers. They felt as out of place as we did.

They began to walk the grounds in their robes and slippers as if it were the fashion. On top of that, we had mistakenly scheduled a group of fire dancers to perform at 2 P.M. on the opening day. The performance might've been okay had we scheduled it in the evening beneath the dark night sky, but it fizzled under the afternoon sun in front of the robe-wearing crowd.

These failures led to an epiphany. People had not come for the plush spa attire or fire dancers or to be in the GQ Room. They'd come to meet new people. Everybody was having a blast simply bumping into each other in the hallways. We were introducing attendees who were focused on the bottom line to people who were working to make the world a better place. As it turned out, they had a lot to learn from each other.

This became clear when Mikkel Vestergaard Frandsen took the stage. He lived to stop disease. Everyone was on the edge of their seats when he said it was only a matter of time before we had another pandemic like the Spanish flu of 1918. (How right he turned out to be.) Mikkel grabbed everybody's attention for two reasons: His information was cutting-edge, and he was a businessperson whose business *helped* people. He wasn't running a charity. His companies were for-profit *and* saved lives.

Mikkel's businesses operated out of Switzerland. In addition to producing mosquito nets treated with insecticide that prevented the spread of malaria, he was also the inventor of the LifeStraw filtration devices, which removed almost all bacteria, microplastics, and parasites from contaminated water. Mikkel's companies were helping to save millions of lives, and he was making a very comfortable living doing so.

"You can do well by doing good," he said. "This is humanitarian entrepreneurship." Everyone was enthralled. Although corporate social responsibility is prevalent now, at the time it was barely a blip on the radar of most young tech start-ups. That didn't mean our attendees didn't want to make a difference; they just had to be shown that it was possible to do so without leaving their business aspirations behind.

Blindly writing a check to the Red Cross was not nearly as interesting to them as working with thought leaders like Ellen Gustafson and Lauren Bush. While some of our attendees understood the value of domain names, others ran companies attempting to stop child trafficking. The heads of Invisible Children, an organization that promoted awareness and advocacy to protect kids in Uganda who were abducted and forced into becoming soldiers, were bumping into Silicon Valley's leading tech founders. Everybody was learning no matter which way they turned.

Later that day, our audience was taken to an unexpected place when Ethan Zohn, the winner of the reality show *Survivor: Africa,* stood up to give his talk.

As a contestant, Ethan had been allowed to bring one personal item of his choice to remote Africa. Having been a professional soccer player, he chose to bring his hacky sack. It was the only thing that brought him joy during the difficult *Survivor* experience. After one challenge, Ethan found himself kicking around the hacky sack with a group of barefoot children in a hospital parking lot. The kids had no soccer ball, so to make one, they'd wrap twine around some rags. Ethan's hacky sack thrilled these kids so much that he gave it to them when he left.

Before he departed, he asked a nurse why those kids were playing in a hospital parking lot. The nurse explained that the children were infected with HIV. The disease was being passed on from mother to infant in many sub-Saharan countries, where one in every twenty people tested positive.

Ethan decided to take his million-dollar prize money from winning *Survivor* to start the organization Grassroot Soccer. He wanted to provide kids with soccer equipment and playing fields, and connect young people with mentors, information, and health services to help combat the AIDS epidemic in Africa. "Find out what makes your heart break," he loved to say, "and join an organization that does something about it."

Everyone in the room stood up and applauded. After that long standing ovation, Elizabeth Gore stepped onto the stage to speak about the charity auction we would soon host. She announced that the winner would have dinner with Ted Turner and all proceeds would go to the UN Foundation and Nothing but Nets.

When Elizabeth had first suggested the auction to us, we were thrilled with the idea. *An auction at the St. Regis for charity?* we thought. *We could really raise a lot of money here.*

The problem was, we had never seen a real auction. All we knew was to talk fast, get the highest price, and then say, "Going once, going twice, sold!"

So Elliott and Jeff stood up to co-host the bidding, but they didn't really know where to start the pricing, and they certainly weren't prepared for the awkward moment when nobody bid. After a long, excruciating silence, one of the tech entrepreneurs threw out a small offer, perhaps out of pity. After even more silence, Mikkel jumped in and placed his own five-figure bid. The crowd gasped.

The tech entrepreneur fired back with an even higher bid.

Mikkel just as quickly returned the serve with a new bid that crept into the six-figure range. The tech entrepreneur smiled and bowed out, Elliott got to use his "Going once, going twice, sold" line, and the crowd erupted for Mikkel.

After the claps subsided, the runner-up stood up in the

back and asked to speak. We sent a microphone out to him, and he pledged to donate $75,000. He wasn't even bidding on anything—he just wanted to support the cause.

"I don't even know who Ted Tiggel is," he said, his words clearly making his point. "I just want to get involved."

The room erupted once more, and in that moment we realized we were on to something.

Attendees took to Twitter to raise even more funds for the UN Foundation. Elizabeth couldn't believe what she was seeing as she watched the tweets roll in. At the time, using Twitter to raise money was a novel approach to fundraising. But people in the room were doing more than giving money or encouraging others to donate over the Internet. They were thinking about how to change their own business models to help other people.

It was as if everybody had discovered the double bottom line: doing well *and* doing good.

By the end of the event, we'd raised $250,000 for the UN Foundation, and Elizabeth Gore was ecstatic. She would start other campaigns at future Summit Series events, including Girl Up, a movement to advance girls' skills, rights, and leadership opportunities. For us, we'd found our sweet spot: We wanted to be the mortar between the for-profit and nonprofit worlds and influence people to use their success to better society.

We had raised a quarter of a million dollars for charity, and we knew we could do it again, because, for the first time, *we* had a double bottom line. Not only had we helped the UN Foundation, but our event had sold enough tickets to make a slight profit.

On the final morning, we thanked everyone for being

there and said our goodbyes. After three nonstop days of running around the event, we should have been exhausted. But we were too excited to sleep. We had finally figured out what we wanted Summit Series to be. Now we needed to make our new vision a reality.

14

YOU DON'T GET CHANCES,
YOU TAKE THEM

The idea of returning to Brett's grandmother's condo in Florida made it seem, in a way, as though we were landing back where we'd started. But now we felt like completely different people. In the past few months, we'd not only pulled off a last-minute event at the White House and raised a large sum of money for charity in Aspen but also developed a solid understanding of our own values. We knew how we wanted to run Summit Series and the type of community we wanted to build. We no longer saw ourselves as simply a series of ongoing events; rather, we thought of ourselves as providing a platform to foster a community based on thought leadership, collaboration, and kindness. We felt our name no longer embodied our newly defined vision, so we dropped the "Series" and rebranded ourselves simply as "Summit."

Once we had discovered a Florida retirement home wasn't the aspirational headquarters we had in mind, we took our small profit from the event in Aspen, pushed it back out onto the table, and gambled that we could find a way to do something that would put ourselves on the map in New York City.

We pooled our resources and moved into a cramped, white-walled apartment in Lower Manhattan, complete with children's bunk beds and mattresses on the floor. Not exactly the lap of luxury we had just experienced at the St. Regis, but we were too eager to keep building on our momentum to care.

We ate dinner from our neighborhood bodega, which served food off hotplates. We could've each had our own bedroom across the river in Hoboken for the same rent, but we decided we'd rather be at the center of the action. The only problem was our version of "the center" didn't include Internet service.

"Jeremy, how do we get on the Wi-Fi?"

Jeremy had officially become the tech guru on top of everything else he did. He'd mastered piano, drums, guitar, and the music software Pro Tools, so we just assumed he could do everything else. In addition to adding technology to his growing list of responsibilities, he also set up a video editing studio in the laundry closet to put together sleek-looking videos from the Aspen event; with a nod to the smell of detergent, he called that tiny space the "Downy Editing Bay."

We took up to seven meetings a day in order to grow our community, meeting with entrepreneurs who shared our values. That also helped us stay fed—often the people we met with were older and more successful, so they felt inclined to treat us to the meal. When we hosted dinners at local restaurants, we had to pass the hat. One time we split the check twenty-six ways (and apologized profusely to our very patient and understanding waiter).

Another benefit of meeting captivating business minds every day was that it accelerated our learning process. Each night, we would bring the best of those experiences back home to share insights with each other.

Despite our perceived success at the White House and Aspen, we still felt naive and clueless. So we were overwhelmed when we got introduced to President Clinton's nonprofit.

We learned that the older generation that had been in power was beginning to notice the new generation of entrepreneurs coming to the world's attention. The Clinton Foundation wanted to connect with these emerging leaders on behalf of the former president. They'd gotten wind of us through the White House event and wondered if we could help. So we offered to throw a charity event for them.

There was only one catch: the fee for Clinton's appearance was a $250,000 donation to the foundation. At the time, the foundation was running several programs, from eradicating HIV/AIDS to providing disaster relief to combating climate change. We were all for that, but in order to contribute, we needed to figure out how we were going to raise the money. We could barely afford bodega sandwiches, let alone a quarter-million-dollar donation.

But we soon discovered a small loophole.

If we'd gone through the speakers bureau that represented President Clinton, we would've been forced to pay all the cash up front. But because we were fortunate enough to be dealing with some trusting people at his foundation, we didn't need to come up with the full payment until the event—just a deposit. This gave us a way out *and* a way in.

We had just raised $250,000 to help rid the world of malaria. What if we used an auction to cover the costs of Clinton's speaking fee? It was the highlight of the event in Aspen. Why couldn't it work in New York?

Bolstered by our last fundraiser, we booked two hours of Bill Clinton's time. We did this without having a concrete idea of how we were going to pay for it all—just enough naiveté to think we'd figure it out along the way.

We planned the event for July 2009. Our goal was to bring together eighty amazing people yet again. But we were worried that repeating the same experience in a different location was going to feel stale. We didn't want to put on the same event over and over again. We wanted to continually release a new product.

Elizabeth Gore taught us that diversity of thought makes conversations exponentially better, so we wanted to fill our event with not only entrepreneurs but artists, writers, and musicians as well. As another one of our sayings goes: The more diverse the inputs, the more complex and impactful the outputs. It's a creative numbers game. The more unexpected ideas you hear, the greater the possibility they'll lead to something unexpected.

If we wanted to build the best events, we needed to create a diverse A-list—a pool of people who would be as excited chatting with the CEO of YouTube as they would brainstorming ways to fund education programs in South America. As it turned out, Bill Clinton was the key. Everyone was interested in meeting the former president. An invitation to the event was so enticing that people were calling us to ask if they could bring an extra guest. And those extra guests were often even higher-profile than the person we had originally invited.

One of the attendees offered us their $20 million apartment to throw the event, and soon guests began to offer to bring prominent leaders from the entertainment industry. While we had deliberately used the friends-and-family strategy to make Aspen work, now it was happening naturally without us even having to ask.

It also allowed us to mend relationships with people who'd been upset by Elliott's Aspen email. We were aware of how badly we'd screwed up, and we tried to reach out to each person who'd been offended. It helped that the event would once again be free to attend.

"Look, I know you haven't taken my call in two months. But I'd like to invite you to spend an evening with Bill Clinton," we said. We told them they'd be joined by Adrian Grenier, Blake Lively, Kirsten Dunst, Wyclef Jean, and Adriana Lima. "It's going to be a great evening."

The New York Times caught wind and wrote a story about us in the business section. We laughed when we picked up a copy and saw Elliott referred to as *"Mr.* Bisnow." Nobody knew we were surviving by the skin of our teeth. We needed to run that charity auction like our lives depended on it— because, frankly, our credit cards *did* depend on it.

The strategy for the auction began to take shape during a late-night brainstorming session in our tiny apartment. Could Wyclef bring a winner to his recording studio? Yes! Would Adrian take a winner onto the set of *Entourage*? Yes! Did we know anyone who could donate World Cup tickets? Yes! Did we know anyone who could donate a zero-gravity parabolic airplane flight? Weirdly enough, yes! Would all that cover the $250,000 we owed the president? . . . No clue!

That's when we had an idea. We recalled Clinton's appearance in sunglasses playing the sax on *The Arsenio Hall Show* in 1992, which endeared him to the American public and helped him win the presidency.

So we bought two $150 saxophones. Our hope was if we needed a trump card at the auction, we could pull out the instruments—which we'd get the president to sign—to get us over the line.

But even if that worked, we still wouldn't have the money until the night of the event. President Clinton's appearance at our event was essentially going to need to be paid for . . . by his appearance at our event.

We needed a financial base. We knew of people who really wanted to attend the event and were happy to write a check to support us. At first we were reluctant to ask. We felt embarrassed. Here we were producing a high-profile event for the former leader of the free world, and we had to resort to begging for money to help us pull it off. But if you don't ask, you don't get. So we put our egos aside and reached out to our supporters. We got ten people to pay $10,000 each for a ticket, and crossed our fingers that the sign of goodwill would be enough to placate the president's people.

Elliott took the subway up to the former president's office in Harlem to talk about the schedule with his team. "Yeah, and about that deposit . . ." Elliott said. "We don't have all the cash at the moment. Can we give you $100,000 for now? That will give us time to put the event together in order to make the whole donation."

Clinton's people were understanding, albeit somewhat apprehensive, and Elliott left the two saxes with them to be signed.

At the same time, Jeff and Brett were walking to a food festival at Bryant Park. We needed a culinary concept for the event. Because President Clinton was on a health kick after his quadruple bypass surgery, we thought it would be apt to find a celebrity chef who could make a vegan meal.

Jeff had caught wind that Tom Colicchio was cooking at the food festival. Colicchio was the founding chef of Gramercy Tavern, which had been voted the most popular restaurant in New York City three times. *What the hell,* Jeff thought, *it can't hurt to ask.*

Jeff and Brett went to the park expecting a farmer's market but encountered a buttoned-up event closed to anyone without a credentialed badge. There were guards and security checkpoints, and neither Jeff nor Brett had a name to drop. So they did what any cash-strapped person in their early twenties would have done: They jumped a fence and found their way over to where Colicchio was leading a demo for some VIPs.

"All right, Jeff, let's keep a low profile," Brett said. "I say we slowly move in from the side. As soon as he finishes this demo, we'll—"

"Mr. Colicchio!" Jeff called out. "We'd love to invite you to cook for President Clinton!"

Startled but intrigued by the offer, Colicchio paused mid-demonstration, turned toward Jeff and Brett, and shouted back: "Sounds amazing."

"It needs to be vegan!" Brett jumped in.

"He had heart surgery," Jeff added.

"I love a challenge. Call my people."

And just like that, Colicchio was on board to cook a vegan feast.

We might have had the food covered, but we were still deep in a financial hole. We woke up the morning of the event knowing we needed to raise $150,000 to cover the remainder of Clinton's speaking fee for his foundation. And to pull it off, we were putting all our faith in two $150 saxophones.

15

FORTUNE FAVORS THE BOLD

Oriental rugs and plush, oversize couches filled the penthouse living room. Intricate works of art hung in between floor-to-ceiling windows that overlooked the skyline of downtown Manhattan, while the faint sounds of the city below buzzed with excitement in the warm summer evening air.

One by one, attendees strolled out of the elevator into the palatial apartment. There was a palpable buzz in the air as guests connected with each other. Part of the excitement was due to the caliber of people in the room—but realistically, most of it was the knowledge that they were about to meet a former president.

For weeks we'd been on the phone, casually asking our attendees if they'd like to meet the president. But behind our nonchalant facade was the truth: We had never met the president either, and we were just as excited as everyone else. We took pride in our ability to think on the fly and form connections between like-minded strangers—but when one of those strangers used to be one of the most powerful people on the planet, there isn't a playbook to turn to.

"As you know," the president's chief of staff told Elliott, "you'll be introducing the president to your guests. Please tell the president who they are and what they do so they can connect."

Elliott had memorized each person's bio on the guest list. He was as prepared as he could be, but as soon as the president came through the door, he forgot all his polished lines. Elliott was so disarmed that he had no choice but to be himself. He went over to say hello, and suddenly, now he *had* met the president. He felt a strange sense of confidence wash over him.

As the photo line began to assemble, Elliott stood between the president and each guest, making small talk and doing introductions. With each conversation, Elliott realized something existential: He was no longer Casino-Floor Elliott. He had evolved. Suddenly, all of the people who approached them were reverent—not only toward the president but toward Elliott as well. Nobody had ever treated him like this before.

"Stephen, so glad you and President Clinton are finally going to get a chance to talk . . ."

"Mr. President, this is Jessica Jackley, the co-founder of the micro-lending platform Kiva."

"Wyclef, so good to see you. Let me introduce you to the president."

"Mr. President, I really want you to meet my mentor . . ."

We'd woken up that morning on bunk beds—but that's not how the founder of YouTube saw us as we introduced him to the president. We were connecting highly successful people who'd never met one another, and in doing so, we felt elevated to their same level of success, even though we were subsisting on bagels. We were no different than when we'd rolled out of bed that morning, but we were *perceived* differently, and that made us feel different.

When the photo line finished, the President got ready to address the group. People were sitting on the floor, on sofas, on the back of sofas, behind the sofas ... nobody wanted to be more than thirty feet away.

It's often said that Bill Clinton has a way of making everybody in the room feel like he's talking only to them, and maybe that's because he's deeply curious about each and every person he meets. His team told us that when he got up to speak, he would process the interactions he'd had and speak off the cuff to the mood of the room. All he needed was a glass of water and a mic.

We found out why Bill Clinton was called "the Michael Jordan of public speaking" at that time. It was more than just articulating a bright vision for the future. He was able to connect that vision with our hopes for what Summit might one day become and deliver it with the finesse of a rehearsed presidential address.

He stressed that the only constant is change, but change can be scary to people who are holding on to old values or views. These people see the world through a lens of competition, but what they really need is to rely more on each other. The more we could collaborate, the more we could make ourselves indispensable. Building positive interdependence, he said, is what creates more alliances, peace, understanding, and abundance.

It was like hearing a State of the Union written especially

for us. It was deep and meaningful, and everyone let him know how grateful they were with a shoulder-to-shoulder standing ovation.

The president stayed for twice as long as he had scheduled. But as soon as he left, we noticed some of the crowd started getting ready to head home, too.

That was not good. We still needed to come up with $150,000 to pay the president, and our auction hadn't started yet. Our stomachs began to churn.

"Before we wrap up for the evening," Jeff quickly announced, "we're really excited to present an amazing opportunity to do something truly meaningful for a great cause ... Let's get started with the charity auction!"

Nobody had any idea there was going to be an auction, aside from the few who had offered to donate items. We tried to wrangle our confused guests back into place so we could quickly begin the bidding process.

Much to our relief, the crowd seemed to like the items we had cobbled together and found our bravado entertaining. People started enthusiastically bidding on the recording session with Wyclef or the visit to the set of *Entourage* with Adrian Grenier. But by the time we ran through all of the auction items outside of the two saxophones, we had only brought in $70,000. We were still $80,000 away from meeting our responsibilities. Even if we split that debt four ways, that was $20,000 on each of our credit cards—and the bank hadn't exactly extended that line of credit to us yet. What's more, even if we could convince someone to give us a loan, we had no idea how we would pay it back.

That's when we brought out our trump card: one of the saxophones with Bill Clinton's signature. Elliott started the bidding—and he was really pushing it. But there were fewer saxophone aficionados in the room than we'd hoped, and the number of bidders soon dwindled.

Elliott had no choice but to kick it into high gear. He started talking about all the wonderful work that the Clinton Foundation was doing, and mentioned that these donations would be going toward great causes, from protecting children in Africa from malaria to helping companies fight climate change.

"C'mon! Who wants to save the world?" It was a not-so-subtle cry to the group that we needed saving ourselves.

Mikkel Vestergaard Frandsen was in the room, our original savior at our first attempt at a charity auction in Aspen. So was Stephen Messer, the former CEO of LinkShare, who had taken a liking to us.

Elliott and Jeff focused on the two of them.

"Can you do $25,000?" Elliott called out to Stephen. Then, "I know you've got your eyes on this, Mikkel. Do I hear thirty?"

Mikkel smiled. He was in on our game. He'd already watched us play it before in Aspen.

"Stephen?" The crowd was now cheering Stephen on, and he almost rolled his eyes. "Do we hear thirty-five?" He nodded his head reluctantly.

"Mikkel, did I just hear $40,000 pass your lips? Yes, I did!" Mikkel smiled.

"Stephen, will you do forty?"

He agreed.

Just at the point when we'd pushed them as far as we could, Elliott announced: "Great news! We have an exciting announcement for everyone." He paused to seize the tension. "There are actually *two* signed saxophones, and both bidders will get one!"

The room roared with laughter. By this time, it seemed like everybody in the room was in on it.

"Let's give Stephen and Mikkel a huge round of applause. Forty thousand dollars each! Eighty thousand to charity! You are both champions!"

We had used the auction to pull together the final $150,000 that would go toward the Clinton Foundation—*and* we were off the hook. After that, the rest of the evening was pure relief. We weren't going to go into debt, and we'd just raised a quarter million dollars for charity—again. The following day, President Clinton called Elliott while he and Jeff were on the street. They weren't expecting it. It wasn't a perfunctory thank-you either. The president actually wanted to know how we were doing.

President Clinton wanted to chat.

We were so stunned, we didn't know how to reply. The only thing Elliott could think to say was, "Things are good. How are Hillary and Chelsea?"

Three months earlier, we had been relying on the pity of our mentors to keep us fed. Now, Elliott and Jeff were chatting with the president the way they would any of their friends.

Finally, we felt like we belonged in the room.

It seemed we had finally made a splash in New York. The natural thing for us to do would have been to stick it out in the city. To milk the momentum we had just created and bask in the success of what we had pulled off. But we were firm believers in growth over comfort, and we felt we had stretched ourselves as far as we could in Manhattan.

So with what little money we had left from our Aspen event profits, we decided it was time to hit the road. Little did we know just how uncomfortable things were about to get.

16

THROW OFF THE BOWLINES

nspired by Tim Ferriss's bestselling *The 4-Hour Workweek,* we spontaneously bought one-way tickets to Central America and bounded off.

Tim's book is filled with tips on how to set up your business in a remote place abroad where you can get the most out of your dollar. There was very little in those 424 pages to prepare us for the scorpions and lightning storms that were coming our way, but it did teach us something even more valuable: *Throw off the bowlines.* The line originates from a Mark Twain quote. The bowlines refer to the ropes that hold a ship safely to the dock, and the idea is that by cutting ties with the safety of shore and sailing off into the ocean despite the risk, one can find new discoveries and adventures. Similarly, we felt that once you leave the comforts of home, you open yourself up to new opportunities and can stretch yourself to evolve into somebody new. If you stay comfortable, you won't discover new parts of yourself. And we knew the unworldly selves who were sleeping in bunk beds in New York weren't the ones we wanted to continue being.

Brett and Jeremy had found a *finca* on the southwest coast of Nicaragua that seemed almost too good to be true. *Finca* means "farm" in Spanish, but unbeknownst to us, in Central America it is also a loose term for wilderness. We stared out the window in amazement as our shuttle drove along a long dirt road just outside the town of San Juan del Sur. Howler monkeys greeted us as we arrived at our secluded home on a hill.

As soon as the shuttle came to a stop in the driveway, we raced inside, excited to bask in our beautiful new home for the next few months. The house was perched high on the hillside with expansive views overlooking the entire town of San Juan del Sur and a vibrant blue ocean in the background. A sprawling pool stretched through the center of the property with several large bedrooms huddled around it.

We couldn't believe how lucky we were to have found this place.

We were thrilled to have traded the concrete jungle of Manhattan for real jungle in the tropics. But as we sat around the kitchen determining who would get which bedroom, we were interrupted by some uninvited guests.

Ants. Not a few ants in a column. We're talking about *millions of ants* in a swarm so thick they looked like a carpet rolling its way toward us from the bushes, over the patio, into the house, up the walls, and onto the ceilings—all in a matter of minutes.

"What the hell is that?"

"I've never seen anything like this in my life!"

"How are we going to stay here?"

Ten minutes later, as if on cue, all of the ants packed up

and retreated back to the bushes as if they had never been there at all. The four of us stared at each other blankly, then shared a sigh of relief. We continued looking around the majestic home, which was costing us less than $16 a day each. The elation resumed, but tinged with a buggy hesitancy.

"Well, it's better than Boca Raton!"

"We can adapt, right?"

"Let's just stick it out."

We took turns exploring, reporting back on the spiders, beetles, and praying mantises. Everywhere we turned there was a new discovery.

"Has anybody noticed there's a forty-pound toad in our swimming pool?"

"Can anyone still hear that howler monkey?"

"Ah, we'll get used to it. Welcome to the jungle, baby."

Anytime one of us started to wimp out, the other three would jump all over him and tell him to step it up. Then, as we unpacked in our rooms, the calm was shattered by the piercing slam of a door.

Jeremy had opened his closet to put his clothes away and been greeted by a scorpion on the door inches from his nose. He leapt back and kicked the door shut.

"Okay, that's it! This isn't going to work," he exclaimed. "We're going to find a place that doesn't have the word *finca* in the title."

We got in touch with the very understanding owner of the house, who referred us to a broker. Much to our relief, the broker pointed us toward a four-bedroom home on the peninsula outside San Juan del Sur. It had a breathtaking view over the entire bay, which opened into the Pacific Ocean. Simply tasting the salt in the air gave us the feeling that anything was possible.

But we weren't just here for a holiday. We were here to work.

Once we settled into our new home, we quickly got into a rhythm and realized how hyper-efficient we became without the usual distractions. We put in long hours and got a lot accomplished, all the while surfing, eating healthy, and diving into books like *Be Here Now* by Ram Dass and travelers' classics like *The Alchemist* and *Shantaram*. We got introduced to meditation; talked about ideas big and small, practical and crazy, late into the night; and truly bonded. Instead of moving from meeting to meeting in New York City and reacting to opportunities, we spent time thinking about our long-term vision for Summit and focused on creating our next event.

We were aiming to scale our next gathering to 250 attendees, and we landed on South Beach in Miami for the location. Brett loved it when people called to ask what he was up to: "Well, I'm overlooking the water in San Juan del Sur and working on our next event . . . what about you?"

We felt so at home that we began to invite people to visit us. Tim Ferriss was the first. It only seemed fair to invite the person who had inspired us to cut the bowlines in the first place. He came down to work on his next book from our oasis. That month gave us a huge confidence boost. His book had pointed us toward what *he* had found, and now we were pointing him toward what *we* had found. We began to sense how we could impact lives.

It was a time of great personal growth. We were open to each other's thoughts, and that was crucial when a storm pushed us to take a hard look at what we were creating.

We were surfing one afternoon when we saw a vivid flash of lightning followed by a crack of thunder in the distance.

Electrical storms are beautiful to look at from behind the safety of a windowpane, but out in the open ocean? Not so much.

The four of us huddled up on our surfboards to talk over the dangers. When some of us started to panic, Elliott reassured us that there was no need to worry about our imminent electrocution. We just had to use a simple formula to determine how far the lightning strikes were from us: count the seconds between the lightning flash and the sound of thunder. Every second, according to this formula, meant the lightning was a mile away.

The next time we saw the lightning, we counted five seconds before we heard the lightning. That meant the storm was five miles away—far enough to let us keep surfing. But the next time we saw lightning, it seemed closer, and the thunder sounded two seconds later. According to the formula, the lightning was still two miles away.

This method would have worked well, except we were using the wrong formula. As it turned out, for every second between the lightning and the thunder, the storm is actually one-fifth of a mile away. That explained why the lightning seemed to be striking so ominously from almost directly overhead.

We realized that something was wrong and that we had to get back to land *immediately*. The wind was whipping the crests of the waves into our faces. We frantically hopped back into the tiny tin boat we had rented for the day to access the surf break—in hindsight, maybe not the best material for a boat that day—to motor out of the cove and back to the harbor. The storm was enveloping everything around us. Elliott had his feet on a life preserver, somehow hoping the electricity wouldn't come through it if lightning struck next to the metal boat. When the lightning flashed, it felt like we could feel the hair on our bodies singe.

We cut through the water as fast as our little motor would churn, not knowing when or where the next lightning bolt would strike. It felt like we were playing Russian roulette with the sky. Seconds felt like hours as we crept our way along the shoreline until finally the harbor came into view. Inch by inch, we plowed toward the shoreline as deafening cracks of thunder raged above us. Then, in a burst of joy, we finally reached the dock, handing out hugs of gratitude as we ran inside for shelter, sopping wet from rain, seawater, and fearful sweat.

That moment was a reminder for us to check in with ourselves and the direction we were headed. What couldn't we see on the horizon? What incorrect assumptions were we making? How could something potentially go wrong? Remembering to readjust our formula became an important metaphor as we prepared for our next event in Miami.

One of those readjustments was calling everyone individually to invite them to buy tickets. We'd decided against sending group emails after the Aspen fiasco, and these conversations allowed us to better understand our audience's needs.

One of those calls was to one of our biggest supporters, Michael Chasen, the CEO of the educational company Blackboard, to invite him to our Miami event. Elliott had first met Michael at Dupont Circle in Washington, D.C., years earlier, during his Bisnow Media days. Michael had been dropping some clothes at the dry cleaner just as Elliott was walking back to his windowless office. Elliott recognized Michael and ran over to introduce himself—a cold pitch, out of the blue, at a dry cleaner. A friendship and mentorship developed, and Michael had attended almost every Summit event since. So we assumed he'd be all in for this one.

"I don't want to go," Michael said. His response came out of nowhere like that first lightning bolt. "I've already met amazing people at the last three events. I have enough new relationships to last a lifetime."

He told us that he was happy he'd gone to the earlier events, but that we weren't really growing. In Aspen, we'd had three content sessions in total, all packed into one day. That, he said, was like going to college and getting offered one course.

"If you are going to be a real conference company," Chasen told us, "you need to have content that repeat customers will want to return to every time. Have you seen other events? You can do your own version, but there *is* something to be learned there. You can't just have three sessions over an entire weekend. You've got to give me some real stuff, and a lot of it."

As we hung up the phone we felt slapped in the face. Our immediate reaction was to cling to what had worked in the past.

He just doesn't get what we're doing, we thought. We saw Summit as the anti-conference, a place where people could meet simply to make genuine connections. But Michael was telling us that being an anti-conference wasn't good enough.

If we were back in the United States, we probably would have chalked that conversation up to one guy's opinion and surged ahead regardless. But in San Juan del Sur, we were in a slower, more contemplative mode. We were now reading Eckhart Tolle's *A New Earth.* A big message from Tolle is that you are not your thoughts; you're the observational awareness behind those thoughts. You can choose how to show up at any moment, and you're not limited by your experiences, past wounds, or shortcomings. What you need to do is find the opportunity in each moment. And that's exactly what we did with Michael's feedback.

When we looked carefully at our old formula, we realized he was right. We *did* need content—content that told stories, content that would make people lean in, content that would have an impact. The four of us didn't pretend to have brilliant insights across diverse areas—that brilliance came from our community. But it was our role to spread the community's insights across a wide swath of silos. How could we do that?

When we recalibrated our formula, we decided to move Summit away from an anti-conference and toward an interdisciplinary learning festival. We had to figure out not only how to bring a ton of diverse speakers to our next event but also how to think beyond the stage. We wanted to think about music, art, and culinary experiences as well as intellectual discourse. We carefully picked apart each element of our formula. It was a crucial time in our development.

From that moment on, we were no longer only about gathering entrepreneurs to meet one another. We began to call our attendee base and ask them what kind of content they wanted. We realized that everyone has something to teach and everyone has something to learn. We needed to look at the many disciplines that our community covered and find material that would benefit all of our attendees. We needed to allow them to choose their own adventure.

By taking apart the old formula, we forced ourselves to create many new ones. That brought us face-to-face with one of our biggest weaknesses.

17

YOU HAVE TWO EARS AND ONLY ONE MOUTH. USE THEM IN THAT RATIO

Summit had grown out of our broadening personal networks, and subsequently the personal networks of *those* personal networks. Because we had started as four young, middle-class guys, it meant that as our network grew, it was naturally expanding with other young start-up types.

The situation would've been completely different if we'd begun with two female and two male founders. But the four of us came together as very young and very naive men, and there was no class in college that taught us what it felt like to be female and be underrepresented in many business-related situations. We hadn't done a good enough job of educating ourselves, and now we wanted to not only learn, but enact the lessons we'd failed to understand.

As we looked back at our events, the numbers told a harsh truth. The last three gatherings we produced had comprised fewer than 20 percent women. The statistics were undeniable, and we couldn't move forward without acknowledging them. We needed to create an environment that women would feel more welcome in. We needed to recalibrate our formula for gender balance and inclusion. But the truth was, we didn't know how.

We deeply wanted our events to have a better gender balance. But this wasn't a problem that could be solved using the same methods with which we pursued our other challenges. There wasn't a different catering option or sound-system setup that solved for male entitlement. When it came to diversity and belonging, we needed to make a major change.

That's not something you can do with the snap of your fingers. It's not going to happen by sending an email or calling a meeting in a conference room. There need to be major foundational shifts, and that takes time. We needed to have started years before.

We began asking our women friends to tell us what we were doing wrong and how we could improve. We learned that many of them were disappointed that so few women attended our events and that we didn't have any women on our team. We also learned about the content and experiences female leaders wanted, and how we were failing to provide it. We realized it was important for us to create an environment where the women who came to our events felt valued and included.

We knew we needed to make a major shift before our next event in Miami. We owed it to our community to do better.

That's when an unexpected opportunity surfaced—one that could help turn around our situation.

We were on a call with the tequila brand Patrón, exploring a sponsorship opportunity for our Miami event. They told us, to our disappointment, that they couldn't give us any cash for the partnership, but they'd be happy to donate their product. As the call wrapped up, they mentioned, almost in passing, that they could throw in an additional perk.

They told us they had access to a train car that we could use for a day to host an event for twenty people. And it wasn't just any old carriage: It was a 1927 vintage railcar whose owner, the founder of Patrón and billionaire John Paul DeJoria, had spent $2 million to renovate. There were three state rooms and an observation room with beautiful textiles and hand-carved woods. It looked like something a sultan would have used to travel through Bali a century ago.

They told us that the train car, which was currently parked in Los Angeles, could be hooked onto the back of any regularly scheduled Amtrak train and would ride like a caboose. If we wanted it, we could take it for a trip down to San Diego and back. And we could have it for free.

We were thrilled. It was ours for a day. We just needed to figure out what to do with it.

Then we realized this was the perfect time to start righting our wrongs. We could create a unique experience, and devote it to female entrepreneurs in the hopes that everyone involved would feel special. So we set out to gather twenty female leaders from the business, arts, and nonprofit worlds who could learn from each other and build friendships.

Now *we'd* be four men at an event with twenty women. How would that make us feel? While we might be uncomfortable on the other side of gender imbalance, we'd also be four novices in a room filled with twenty leaders who had already made a huge impact in the world, and from whom we could humbly learn.

In addition to the train ride, we decided to organize an

adventure for our group around the harbor in San Diego. Jeff's soccer teammate back at American University had a boat-leasing business there, and he found us a sailboat to rent on the cheap. We could enjoy the water for an hour and a half before the return trip.

Women who'd lifted us up before, like Elizabeth Gore, helped assemble an all-star crew. The people on the guest list were deeply passionate about helping to shape the next generation of women who would follow in their footsteps. They included:

KRISTEN BELL: The actor who'd later go on to inspire millions of girls as the voice of Anna in the animated film *Frozen*.

ALEXIS JONES: An activist who started a nonprofit called I Am That Girl that had 276 chapters around the world fighting the ideas of perfectionism that many young girls have to confront.

NOA TISHBY: An actor and a producer of *In Treatment* on HBO, and a mentor for women in film.

KATE LEE: The ICM literary agent and Medium executive who had a huge impact in the book publishing world when she brought the first Internet writers into it.

We said goodbye to our home in Nicaragua and jumped on a flight to Los Angeles. By the next afternoon, we were greeting guests on the train platform. That's when we first realized just how much we had to learn—and we got schooled.

The differences in the way we showed up were stark from the outset. The twenty women were elegantly dressed, while Elliott arrived in tennis shorts and Crocs and Jeremy was wearing ripped jeans.

On top of that, as we boarded the train and left the station heading toward San Diego, we noticed that many of the conversations that sprang up around us were very different from the conversations we might have started ourselves. They were nuanced and deeply vulnerable.

Our minds flashed to all those huge tech events that were generally 80 percent men—conferences that Summit resembled—and the types of conversations that often took place in the hallways there. We realized we wanted to create a different kind of event, one that provided an environment that allowed everyone's experience to unfold the way each individual wanted. It was our job to create a canvas that was as attractive, comfortable, and representative to women as it was to men.

On the train ride back to Los Angeles, we realized that it was no longer our place to be in the room. We wanted to give the women an opportunity to relax without these four awkward guys there. So we excused ourselves and walked out the back door to give them space.

It was like a scene out of Wes Anderson's *The Darjeeling Limited*. We were hanging off the back of the caboose with the wind rushing through our hair, traveling a hundred miles an hour up the coast. We could barely hear each other talk, but in the end, we didn't have to say a word.

We now understood how we had to create space for others. And because we had moved aside, it finally felt like we were moving forward.

18

CULT CLASSIC, NOT BESTSELLER

There is an ancient Chinese proverb that says, "The best time to plant a tree was twenty years ago. The second-best time is now."

All the readjustments we'd made over the summer in Central America were integrated into our event in Miami in November 2009. That didn't mean these changes were evident for all to see. It's like planting a tree. You don't see anything at first because the growth is happening underground. The roots are expanding. Then, after a while, a sapling pops up. By year three, you can see it growing quickly.

Having the ability to understand this concept of patience is crucial for any business, especially when you might just barely be surviving until the tree yields fruit.

We were aware that our last event in Aspen had felt a little stiff, so we wanted to make our next one as carefree as possible. We wanted people to feel like they were on vacation, to give them a taste of the freedom we felt in San Juan del Sur. At the same time, we wanted to use the Miami event to expand our offerings and give women a chance to push forward their initiatives.

That's why we decided to book the Ritz-Carlton in Miami's South Beach. To be clear, it wasn't one of the company's trophy properties. It would go through a renovation several years later, but at the time, it offered just the right frame for what we needed to create—that blank, maybe slightly dilapidated canvas on which we could invite people to paint. (Not literally, but the hotel *did* need a paint job.)

We'd doubled our attendees from 120 in Aspen to 250 in Miami. That meant double the costs, too. But there's a direct correlation between creative solutions and a lack of capital.

We couldn't afford to pay for dinner for 250 people at the Ritz. So for one of the evenings, we rented an affordable Art Deco house a quarter mile down the road and had the meal catered. Instead of shelling out money to pay for transportation, we built a parade into the itinerary to try to disguise the ten-minute walk to dinner.

All 250 of us walked from the Ritz over cobblestone streets through the old neighborhood to the dining venue on Española Way. It was drizzling, so many attendees bonded by sharing umbrellas with people they'd never met. The buoyant spirit of the group made onlookers on the sidewalks want to join. It was special to everyone in the moment—but it was much larger than the moment. In fact, it was the genesis for all the dinner parades to follow over the next decade, including the legendary one led by musician Jon Batiste playing a melodica on a mountaintop years later.

We started to experiment with breaking the model of what a conference could be. Did it have to be in a conference room? Did we even *need* a conference room? We assembled a team-based scavenger hunt for our attendees all around

South Beach—the guy who designed it buried himself in a box on the beach, and the winning team had to dig him out to complete the hunt. After dinner one night, we announced that everyone could go to a local ice cream shop and get unlimited ice cream until closing. It cost us a thousand dollars, but that's a small price to pay for all the smiles produced by midnight gelato.

We expanded our content, though we didn't have the time to prepare the wide array that Michael Chasen was advocating. We'd need to study a lot of marquee events first to figure out what was ideal for us—but Michael *did* end up coming to the Miami event. In fact, he was one of our best speakers, alongside the founder of Dropbox, and the president of programming for MTV.

We also invited Elizabeth Gore to unveil the architecture for a campaign called Girl Up, which would support girls around the world striving for social change and gender equality. It was in the idea stage, and Elizabeth didn't want Girl Up to be seen as UN-centric and bureaucratic. We therefore set up a half-day workshop at the Miami event to assist Girl Up with branding. Now, more than a decade later, Girl Up has helped 85,500 girls in 120 countries.

There were also more women at this event than ever before. Many of the leaders on the Patrón train came and brought their friends. On top of that, they helped us put together one of our most highly attended talks at the event, called "Empowering Women Right Here, Right Now: Developing a Game Plan to Overcome the Challenges Facing Twenty-First-Century Women."

Through them, we also began to meet women who would go on to become paramount to our success, like former professional soccer player and Stanford engineer Natalie Spilger.

Natalie would become one of our first team members and a critical part of our Summit family.

All this growth was invisible to many of the attendees who were scavenging around the beach and laughing over ice cream. But we now had a vision for creating an innovative and impactful ideas festival, the likes of which we had never experienced before.

Even the way our hotel rooms looked when the event ended represented how far we had come. At previous events, we had merely relied on the production equipment provided by the hotel, but now we had begun to accumulate our own property rather than borrow others'. All of our hotel rooms were filled wall-to-wall with items from the event: Summit flags, program booklets, boxes of leftover Patrón. There was so much stuff we couldn't even walk around our rooms; we kept DO NOT DISTURB signs on the door the whole time so the staff wouldn't have to navigate around our mess. We had no idea where to put all these leftover items, let alone where *we* were going next. We realized that we needed to measure what we were doing and set a benchmark so we could build upon it moving forward.

Years later, we'd have warehouses on both sides of the country—encompassing tens of thousands of square feet—filled with stages, seating, tents, massive sound systems, pop-up dinner tables large enough to seat hundreds, and hanging chandeliers.

But that was a decade away. Just like authentic inclusivity, it didn't happen overnight. The event in Miami was where the seed was planted for the tree that grew into the Summit of today.

We just needed to give it a little time to grow.

19

LIFE IS A GIVING COMPETITION, AND WE INTEND TO WIN

Our next step was not a step. It was a leap. There is a huge gap between raising money in a charity auction and actually trying to fix the problems directly.

The more our community grew, the more we learned about problems around the world, and how these problems were traditionally left to governments and large charity organizations to deal with—which typically meant they went unresolved.

We began to wonder if the network we were creating could come up with new perspectives, and even solutions. We didn't want to be armchair activists. We wanted to have a mission with meaning, even if we didn't know precisely what that mission was.

Shortly after our event, Jeff was invited to Uganda. We had just helped raise money in Miami for a nonprofit called Invisible Children, and Jeff wanted to see how that money would positively impact local communities. There he got a close look at what the United Nations had called "the world's largest neglected humanitarian emergency."

Uganda had endured a civil war that put millions of people into internment camps. Even after the main conflict came to a halt, the violence didn't end—a warlord named Joseph Kony turned his religious cult into a guerrilla group called the Lord's Resistance Army. His militia abducted thirty thousand children, using many of them as soldiers as it rampaged throughout the region and killed roughly a hundred thousand people.

Two American college students and a recent film school grad traveling through Africa stumbled upon what was going on. They began to make a documentary and presented their videos at high schools, colleges, and churches back home. Ultimately, they created the organization Invisible Children to move the world to action against Kony. Their aims were twofold: to make the names, faces, and stories behind these terrible statistics visible to the world so that Kony would be brought to justice, and to solicit donations and sell merchandise to raise money for humanitarian aid in the afflicted areas.

Jeff was soon on a moped in Uganda with a local teacher who moved from village to village to educate children. The teacher helped abducted kids who'd escaped the jungle reintegrate into their communities, and Jeff visited the handbag factory that Invisible Children had helped build with donations and collaborators from the Summit community.

Jeff walked through a Ugandan warehouse, where hundreds of thousands of dollars' worth of donated food sat on shelves, waiting to be distributed by various humanitarian aid organizations. This food was not getting to the people who needed it, and it was a huge lesson in impotence and impact. Jeff saw that it was young, nimble entrepreneurs who were getting things done—the twentysomething creatives with the film cameras who scaled their programs into farming, education, microfinancing, and more—not the bloated international organizations.

He came back to us with stories of people our age who were trying to stop a war. It inspired us to want to do more than just raise money. Then another mentor stepped in to point us in the right direction.

Through Elizabeth Gore we had connected with Ann Veneman, the executive director of UNICEF and formerly US secretary of agriculture under President George W. Bush, and she was very straightforward with us.

"So, I heard you've raised a ton of money for many of these causes in your generation," she said when we first met her. "I want to help you think about giving in a different way. One trillion dollars has gone into Africa over the past thirty years, and it's gotten poorer. Raising money is not the issue. Your focus should be using the talent of your network on behalf of a few exceptional organizations that are truly solving issues," she said.

She backed up her point by giving us a copy of the book *Dead Aid* by Zambian economist Dambisa Moyo. She also introduced us to the heads of UNICEF Innovation, an arm focused on adapting new technologies and market-based ideas to help those at the bottom of our world's economic structure. Books and conversations like these entirely changed the way we viewed impact.

But there is nothing as eye-opening as being on the ground in a moment of crisis. Unfortunately, we got a chance to see what that was like a few months later when Haiti was rocked by a huge earthquake in January 2010.

Close to two hundred thousand people were killed, a quarter of a million homes were destroyed, and much of the island was reduced to rubble. The catastrophic images we saw broke our hearts. We were still in Miami after our last event, and Haiti was only a one-hour flight from us.

We quickly booked a flight to Port-au-Prince that would depart within forty-eight hours. We didn't know what we were going to do. We just wanted to see what *could* be done.

We started with trying to source basic supplies that kids might need. Over the next two days, we organized a school's worth of supplies from Staples, sourced backpacks and additional supplies from our friends at Incase, and got both freight and personal transport from Project Medishare in Miami. We also asked our friend Mikkel for a community's worth of his LifeStraws that could purify any filthy water to make it drinkable.

When we got there though, we simply weren't prepared for the level of tragedy we encountered. The city had been reduced to rubble. Concrete homes were flipped upside down. Electrical wires dangled from toppled poles. The smell of burnt rubber filled the air from fires scattered throughout the streets. Displaced families were crammed into tent cities as far as the eye could see. Nothing was spared, not even the presidential palace, which had a hole torn through its center. The first time you look upon such damage and turmoil, you begin to understand how much you don't understand. The backpacks and school supplies we'd brought for the kids seemed so trivial against the utter devastation. We spent time with kids, singing and dancing to share small moments of joy with them, but in the end we left them to their tents, feeling like we'd brought a Band-Aid to a fatal wound.

The enormous scope of the damage made us wonder what problems we could confront and how we might try to resolve them in the years to come.

20

DON'T KEEP IT REAL, KEEP IT SURREAL

As we geared up for our next event in Washington, D.C., which we named DC10 to celebrate the start of a new decade, we got an unexpected opportunity to take a short winter break in Montana—and a single day there would change every event we've thrown since. We learned that a little mischief can take you a long way. Sometimes you've just got to listen to your gut and poke your nose where it doesn't belong.

Under normal circumstances, the four of us would never have gotten a chance to lay eyes on the Sugar Shack. That's because it exists beyond the gates of the Yellowstone Club in Big Sky, Montana, which is an exclusive private ski resort.

But we *did* get through those gates, and it was all because we were searching for opportunities anywhere we could find them, from striking up a conversation with the person sitting next to us on a plane to asking a friend to introduce us to someone they had only met for five minutes. This opportunity happened to come from Jeremy's mom, Casey, who had been working for a man in Massachusetts who handled distressed businesses. The Yellowstone Club had hit hard times during the Great Recession, and she had temporarily relocated from Boston to Montana to help run the Yellowstone Club Foundation, the organization's nonprofit arm. Although the club was typically only accessible to members and guests, she told Jeremy she'd be able to get us in to ski.

We all loved to ski. Not only did Summit get started with Elliott's ski trip to Utah, but skiing was one of the foundations of our friendship. Brett started skiing when he was two years old after his dad decided to learn at age forty-three. Jeremy loved the snow and went to school in Colorado for a short time just to be near the mountains. And Jeff and Jeremy first bonded over launching off jumps in a terrain park in New Hampshire. We were always up to hit the slopes.

There was one catch to this opportunity. As we were not members of the Yellowstone Club, Jeremy's mom let us know in very precise terms that we needed to stay under the radar and be on our best behavior.

"Don't worry," Jeremy assured her. "We'll have our ski gear on. Nobody will even know we're here."

Jeremy's mom was still wary, so she put down some detailed ground rules. "Boys," she said, "you're here for one reason—to ski. You can go up after 9 A.M. Make sure you're down before 4 P.M. Do not strike up conversations with anyone on the mountain. Keep your goggles on. Do not go to the lodge. And most of all, whatever you do, do *not* go to the Sugar Shack!"

"The Sugar Shack?"

"The snacks at the Sugar Shack are for the members only," she said. "Do *not* go to the Sugar Shack!"

We nodded gratefully, excited to get out on the slopes.

The next morning as we looked up at the rolling hills and palatial homes, we realized that our matching blue beanies and unkempt facial hair were probably not the best way to go undercover. We felt like we were out of our league. Proper imposters.

As we headed for the lift, Jeremy reminded us: "Let's make sure we're being really respectful of my mom and everything she told us."

The surroundings were perfect: sprawling mountaintops blanketed in snow reaching upward toward crisp blue skies, where covered high-speed lifts whisked skiers swiftly up the mountain. But Elliott had a better idea of how he wanted to spend his day. "Of course we're going to be respectful . . . But I think I just saw Bill Gates walk into the lodge. I'm going to see if I can meet him."

"I'm with Elliott on this one," Jeff said.

"Enjoy, guys. I'm going to ski," Brett said.

"Guys, can everyone just get on the lift?" Jeremy shouted to Elliott and Jeff, but it was too late—they were already working their way toward the lodge, pretending not to hear him. Feeling frustrated and somewhat defeated, Jeremy decided to shrug it off, pop his skis on, and head up on the lift with Brett.

Elliott and Jeff spent the next few hours at the lodge greeting everyone as if they'd been members for years. They tried to meet as many people as they could, while Brett and Jeremy skied for several hours. Eventually, Brett and Jeremy were exhausted.

"I'm starving," Brett said. "I could really use something to eat."

It didn't take long for Brett to find the Sugar Shack, which should be placed in the hospitality hall of fame, and which looked like it could've been made of gingerbread and was right out of the pages of the Hansel and Gretel story; you could smell the most intoxicating aroma of grilled cheese wafting from a hundred feet away.

When you walked in, a staff member warmly greeted you, flipping thin grilled cheeses next to a tureen of heavenly hot chocolate that made you contemplate one of the big questions in life: Should I put in the big marshmallows or the small ones? Every imaginable cookie, candy, or treat was displayed across tables in shimmering glory, and everything was free for the taking (assuming you were a member, of course).

With Elliott and Jeff chatting it up with members at the lodge and Brett and Jeremy sipping some warm tomato soup, it was hard to tell who broke the rules first. But naturally, it was Jeremy's phone that lit up.

"I just got a call saying people have run into my son," his mom said. "How would they know that you're here?"

"Hi! Well, uh, it's funny you mention it . . . everyone's just really friendly up here."

That was actually true. Everyone was warm, welcoming, and happy to chat. One of the best conversations we had was with a guy whose family was one of the first members of the Yellowstone Club, Matt Wiggins. Being the community-oriented person that Matt is, he invited us over for dinner at his beautiful family home, right next to the main ski lift above the main lodge—perfect placement on the mountain. His home had a mud room with enough ski gear for a small platoon and a beautiful kitchen that opened onto the living room and dining area. Near the fireplace stood a narrow, hip-high table, and on it sat an oversized book that looked as if a cartoon fable might jump out when you opened it. It was the family guest book, filled with heartwarming tales told by friends about hanging out there over the years and how much it meant to them.

Wow, Jeff thought. *Could you imagine having people come to your home and have such powerful experiences that they feel compelled to write about it? What a statement on the importance of family, friends, and community.*

Doing the cooking that night was one of Matt's friends, an eccentric chef named Michael Hebb, who was an important figure in the Portland food scene in the early 2000s. Michael stood over the stove, cooking up meat and vegetables with an ardor that we'd never quite seen before.

Jeff immediately became fascinated with Michael and sat down at the kitchen counter as he cooked. Soon the nuggets of wisdom started flying out of Michael. One of them would become a guiding star for us. "You know how people say 'keep it real'?" Michael said.

Jeff nodded slowly, curious as to where Michael was going with this.

"Well, don't do that. You have to keep it *surreal*. You have to go just beyond people's expectations and sense of possibility."

His advice would change the way we conceived our events moving forward. We had already been shaking off many of the expected ways to put on a conference. But Michael's words gave us permission to push the boundaries of what an attendee's experience could be. And our upcoming event in Washington, D.C., DC10, would be the perfect canvas to begin integrating this new belief system.

At DC10, we'd take more chances with the ways we gathered people around the dinner table in order to create a surreal experience. We would set up an experience with Michael in which our guests would receive the provocation to remix the Declaration of Independence. They all would receive copies of the Declaration and a razor blade with their dinner invite, and they were told to chop up the document and re-word it the way they envisioned it should read in their ideal America. We'd host the dinner at a Frank Lloyd Wright house overlooking the Potomac River, allowing the setting to spark deep conversations around topics we might never hear if we simply hosted it at a restaurant.

We'd introduce wellness offerings, a twenty-four-hour snack program (thanks to the inspiration from the Sugar Shack), and late-night food. We'd take people kayaking with an Olympian, foster new relationships for attendees over paintball, and take over the National Mall with a picnic with the founders of Sweetgreen, who would do their first and only large-scale catering project with us. We'd build our own casino with all proceeds going to charity, bring in our biggest speakers to date, and execute on interactive installations. We had a newfound resolve to deliver an experience unlike any-thing that had ever existed.

The ideas for these activations could be traced back to that night in Montana, where the seed of being a modern ideas festival was planted firmly in our minds. We may have skirted around Casey's one request, which was to avoid the Sugar Shack—we have to admit we felt pretty guilty breaking her most basic rule after she had just been so generous and welcoming to us—but by doing so, it opened our minds up to new possibilities and changed the trajectory of our organiza-tion.

We left the Yellowstone Club with a new zeal. We had picked up two new members of our community, Michael

Hebb and Matt Wiggins, and not only that, we had one of those what-if feelings.

What if we could build homes on a mountain like this, tucked away in nature, and fill them with all of our friends? What if we could find our own home as a canvas for our community?

21

DON'T WORRY ABOUT MAKING MISTAKES WHEN YOU'RE MAKING HISTORY

L anding back in Washington was a stark contrast to the crisp, cocoa-filled afternoons we had just enjoyed in Montana. And not just because of the lack of luxury.

With Michael Hebb's advice to keep things surreal, DC10 was quickly becoming infinitely more complex than any event we'd ever done before, and we were so far in over our heads that mistakes seemed to follow our every move.

As 2010 began, there was a lot of excitement around President Obama. So we booked the JW Marriott, a few blocks from the White House, for our May event. No surf. No snow. We were looking for a sense of gravitas. We did keep one constant, though: As usual, we doubled the size of our previous event. Now we were planning for five hundred guests.

In order to attract more attendees, we asked speakers and performers who were not easy to get: people like CNN founder Ted Turner, investor Mark Cuban, Teach for America co-founder and CEO Wendy Kopp, Napster co-founder Sean Parker, Washington, D.C., public schools chancellor

Michelle Rhee, futurist Ray Kurzweil, musician John Legend, and NASA astronauts.

We miscalculated—badly. With four months to go, all of the speakers we reached out to had either declined or were unsure, and we were four hundred tickets shy of our target. The tricks we'd learned up to that point weren't working. Brett decided to turn to the same strategy he'd always used as a teenager when he got in trouble: He called his dad for advice.

The four of us huddled around the speakerphone as Brett laid out the situation to his father. Michael wasn't exactly a seasoned life coach—but he was someone who we trusted to always give it to us straight in the way only a parent can.

"Dad," Brett said, "we're in trouble. We just don't know what to do."

"You're doing it all wrong," Michael said. "You know what your problem is? You're not thinking big enough."

We all looked at one another. Not thinking big enough? Ted Turner. Mark Cuban. Astronauts. "We've already asked all these big names," we said. "How much bigger can we think?"

"You need to think even bigger. You need to get Bill Clinton back. If you get him, everyone will fall into line."

It clicked for all of us as soon as he said it. Brett's dad was right. If we could get Bill Clinton again . . .

We reached back out to the president, and he had an open date. It meant writing another check to the foundation, though. It wasn't an easy decision, but after a lot of back-and-forth, we decided we were okay with it because the money would support good causes through the nonprofit.

Plus, we needed to turn DC10 around—and quick.

So we squared away everything with the former president's team and officially confirmed him for the event. As soon as we did, we immediately called Ted Turner's office. "I'm so sorry. I know you just said no to our event. But we've had a change of plans. President Clinton is confirmed for the keynote. Everyone's talking about the idea of Ted Turner speaking in a keynote slot, as well. Would you reconsider?"

They got right back to us. Yes, Ted Turner was now confirmed.

We went back to Sean Parker's assistant. "We now have Ted Turner and President Clinton. Would Sean like to follow the president? We'd need to know by 3 P.M. today."

Another yes.

We followed up with Mark Cuban. "We have President Clinton and Ted Turner lined up, and we're looking for someone who could keynote the following day. We'd really like it to be Mark."

Bingo.

We set up an interview with John Legend and Wendy Kopp. Kristen Bell was back in. So was Michelle Rhee. The seven astronauts from NASA said yes, yes, yes, yes, yes, yes, and yes.

Our prospective attendees started saying yes, too. In a short period, we reached our goal of five hundred tickets sold. As the event approached, we surged toward 750, and were incredibly excited about some of the people who were attending. Ishmael Beah, author of *A Long Way Gone: Memoirs of a Boy Soldier,* would both attend *and* speak after Jeff learned about his story while he was in Uganda. We were consciously reaching out to up-and-comers who we thought were on the verge of making a huge mark.

Two of those we contacted were business school students at UPenn who were about to revolutionize the eyewear world.

They'd created a company called Warby Parker that broke the mold by selling affordable eyeglasses online instead of expensive frames at the optometrist. Warby Parker allowed customers to order five pairs and try them out for a week before deciding whether to buy them. Not only that, but for every pair sold, money would be donated to a partnering nonprofit that sent glasses to someone in need in the developing world. They were doing for eyeglasses what TOMS had done for shoes.

We loved their business model, so Brett invited cofounders Neil Blumenthal and David Gilboa to expand their connections at DC10.

"Sounds awesome," they replied, "but we're busy."

"You don't understand," Brett pressed, pouring it on. "Unless you're expecting the birth of your first child, you don't want to miss this event."

"We're both graduating from Wharton Business School that weekend."

That normally would've been a showstopper. But Brett pushed on.

"You're gonna graduate and they can mail you the diploma. But you'll never get another chance to come to DC10, and we can't mail you the hundred connections you're going to miss," Brett said. "When is the graduation?"

Graduation was on Sunday.

"Perfect. You can be here at the start on Friday afternoon."

It was a compelling enough argument. They decided to drive down from Philadelphia for the opening. They would make it back in time for graduation, and a budding relationship would grow out of their attendance. A year later, we joined Neil in Jamaica for their first-ever Warby Parker eyeglass drop. We spent the day performing eye exams and distributing hundreds of glasses to those in need, and watched as people's faces lit up when they saw clearly for the first time in their life.

We were so inspired by Warby Parker's business model and commitment to social good that when Neil called Brett to say they were raising their first round of funding, we knew we wanted to be involved. "We don't have much savings," Brett said, "but could we invest what we do have with you guys?" And that's how we became one of the first investors in Warby Parker. All because Brett wouldn't take no for an answer at DC10. You never know where a relationship may lead; often it bears fruit.

Every phone call like Brett's counted. We were sprinting as fast as we could, and we always seemed to be trying to pull a rabbit out of the hat at the last minute, which only increased the tension. What we needed wasn't always more time—it was more people.

We had already tapped Ryan, who was living in D.C. and working on Bisnow Media, to come in and help run operations for the event. But we were still far short of the staffing we'd need. At a typical festival, there's an entire back-of-house production team who you never see but who work twenty hours a day to make sure everything that you *do* see goes off without a hitch. Well, *we* were that production team. We realized we'd need assistance. But instead of hiring a professional outfit, we called in a few favors.

We brought in a couple of people who were handy, and hired some friends to help. Rich Hansen, a talented designer who was instrumental in establishing Summit's brand and identity, worked late into the night piecing together the main stage at the JW Marriott in the final hours before the event.

And when you're tired and racing against the clock, you're not going to be as careful as you should be. Rich grabbed an X-acto knife to open a box—and sliced through his hand. There was blood everywhere. Trouper that he was, he just bandaged it up and kept going. Moments like that cement friendships, and he ended up designing the Uber logo and brand package through connections he made at one of our events.

It felt like we all got bloody knuckles through the night as more and more unexpected obstacles popped up. Some nuts and bolts that were essential for building the stage didn't arrive, and we couldn't find any locally at that hour. We frantically called the company that had shipped the parts from New Jersey, and it had them—but they would need to be driven a few hours south to D.C. The company recommended a limo service that could get them to us quickly. We were staggered when we heard the price. But we had no choice—without those bolts, we'd have no stage for anyone to speak on.

We also had to make sure that all the greenrooms were prepared. We had big-time people joining us, and some of their teams were demanding. This was the first time we'd ever had to deal with contractual riders that had forty-point lists specifying the height of chairs, style of podiums, and brand of products on hand.

On top of that, Yosi Sergant from the White House was calling Elliott again and again, asking if he could orchestrate a bake sale to help an organization that aided the arts. We couldn't have been more grateful to Yosi for bringing us to the White House, and we wanted to help in any way we could. But homemade muffins weren't quite in line with what we had planned.

"I'm so sorry, Yosi," Elliott kept saying, "but I just don't think it makes sense to throw a bake sale in the middle of our event."

With everything swirling around us, there was no time to sleep. Intense moments like these leave you no choice but to rest at the end, not in the middle. We didn't even have time to steam the Summit flags that had arrived wrinkled in their boxes. On the morning of the event, we positioned them onstage as creased as they'd come, and raced to shower and dress.

Before our guests arrived, we took a moment to look around at the hotel we'd transformed, bleary-eyed but smiling proudly. We'd discovered an advantage to working every angle of the event. We knew exactly what had gone into every square inch and what surprises were awaiting the guests. As we met people and toured the area, we exuded an excitement that said, *You have no idea what's in store for you.*

We'd created a music studio in a far corner that had deep blue lighting and felt like a funky recording space in Nashville. There were guitars, keyboards, a full set of drums for attendees to play with, and mics, tambourines, and shakers that allowed everybody to participate. The idea was that Grammy Award–winning musicians and CEOs could jam into the early morning together.

We'd placed massage therapists around the hotel and gave inconspicuous cards to people with instructions to go to specific rooms for acupuncture and stretch therapy. There were fortune cookies filled with the musician Brian Eno's "Oblique Strategies," which are one-liners that get you thinking outside the box: *Ask your body. Remove ambiguities and convert to specifics. Discover the recipes you are using and abandon them*. Elliott's grandmother had baked cookies—sorry, Yosi—and Jeff's grandmother had come all the way from Texas to help her host a session called "Tea with the Grandmas." The event had all of our quirks, but it also had higher caliber guests and more dynamic content than all of the other events put together. It made an announcement to the world: Summit had arrived.

The national news media was there in force, and the mayor of Washington, D.C., opened the event. A few hours later, a detail of Secret Service agents accompanied the former president through the door. A few minutes after that, he was walking out onstage.

"Everyone, please get on your feet and give a huge welcome to the forty-second president of the United States," Elliott announced, pumping up the crowd, "Bill Clinton!"

Elliott held his arms out as if he were in a yoga class and embraced Clinton with a big hug. Any one of the attendees who'd seen awkward Elliott getting heckled after being pulled over by a police car at the first event in Utah only two years earlier had to be in disbelief.

As the president spoke, the four of us sat in the front row, occasionally looking back at the crowd and then at each other. *Can you believe this?* our eyes said. *A former president of the United States is onstage in a packed room right in front of the Summit logo . . . and the flags are wrinkled.*

Our stomachs twisted. Could anyone else see? Were we the only ones noticing? Surely people would be more focused on Clinton than on wrinkled flags—or so we hoped.

As the Clinton session was ending, Elliott went to the back doors that the audience would soon be streaming through. He opened one and peered outside to check the atrium. And there was Yosi, standing in front of a series of fold-out tables that were covered in homemade cakes and cookies.

"*What are you doing?*" Elliott exclaimed.

"I'm having the bake sale I told you about," Yosi said, as calm as could be.

"Yosi, we talked yesterday. We talked the day before. I said you *couldn't* do the bake sale."

"You were wrong."

"What do you mean, I was wrong? *It's our event.*"

"That's okay. You're really young. Everybody makes mistakes. What I'm doing here is for a really important cause."

As he said that, the doors opened, and hundreds of attendees happily and hungrily converged on Yosi's bake sale like bees flocking to honey. How Yosi got past security and set up that bake sale, we'll never know. But we could only stand there and love Yosi for it, realizing that if we had been in his shoes, we would have done the same thing.

Yosi had done to us what he'd done with the "Hope" poster for President Obama when he enlisted Shepard Fairey without the Obama campaign's knowledge. The campaign wasn't too happy with Shepard's first try. But as the second version started appearing at rallies and the walls of college dorm rooms, the campaign had no choice but to acknowledge the boost Shepard's poster had given them. The piece, which was originally based on a photograph by Mannie Garcia, is now in the National Portrait Gallery of the Smithsonian Institution.

"I guess we're having a bake sale!" Elliott said to himself.

In the moment, you tend to overreact to the unexpected. You focus on the missing nuts and bolts, the unexpected oatmeal cookies, and the wrinkled flags. Even if people love 95 percent of what you're putting out, it's human nature to focus on the 5 percent that didn't go as expected and the mistakes you made along the way. That's why when Ted Turner was asked for a piece of advice that would apply to everyone attending, his response became one of our early mantras: "Don't worry about making mistakes when you're making history."

Not only did we feel we were coming closer to fulfilling our goals for what a truly diverse and well-programmed event could be, but we were also on a path to fulfilling Tony Hsieh's suggestion to create a community of people we'd invite to our parents' home for dinner.

And what better person to be the judge of that than our own grandmothers? It felt like nearly every attendee at the event showed up for "Tea with the Grandmas."

Elliott's eighty-four-year-old grandma, Florence, had taken him seriously when he'd asked her to bake a thousand cookies for the session. She'd responded by filling her oven with batch after batch for a week before the event, baking a thousand snickerdoodles.

Then there was Joy Burk, Jeff's grandmother, only four foot eleven but packing a punch, who was pouring tea for all the attendees with the same big bright eyes and interest she'd always displayed during the family dinners she hosted.

Summit was becoming a large extended family. People did not want the party to end. They jammed in the music studio until the break of day. Some of the guests brought the good times to the spontaneous penthouse afterparty in the early morning hours. It was on fire . . . literally—someone accidentally knocked over a high-heat light on the floor and started a small blaze. Thankfully, it was extinguished before we could burn the JW Marriott down. Wrinkled flags, burning drapes—all mistakes we were sure not to repeat.

This time there were no boxes of Patrón stacked in our hotel rooms when DC10 ended. Our small team worked through the final night to break our production down into neatly packaged containers.

Sleep-deprived and happy, we headed off to San Juan del Sur in Nicaragua again the following day—our oasis and the place that invited us to dream. We were all talking about something that Mark Cuban had said onstage: "My life mantra is: 'When I die, I want to come back as me.'"

When people hear that, they think, *Well, of course, he'd want to do that—look at how successful Mark is*. But the point was that Mark had created the mantra *before* he was successful. Even then, he wanted to be living as himself.

All of us embodied that feeling as we sat down at our favorite tiny, open-air restaurant near the ocean in Nicaragua and ordered fish tacos, breathing easy on the other side of our first major conference. DC10 was a landmark for us. The scale of the event and the caliber of speakers had pushed us to another level.

We didn't have a business plan or a ten-year growth strategy laid out. We had never even thought a day further than DC10.

But now it felt like we could do anything.

So we looked at each other and asked: What do we want to do next?

22

NO IDEA SHOULD GO UNSPOKEN

We always gravitated to water, from the beaches of Miami to the surf of Nicaragua. Water aided our creative process; when we were near it, ideas flowed more freely and thoughts seemed clearer.

When we decided we wanted to grow Summit internationally, we didn't seek out the burgeoning tech scene in landlocked Zurich. We made lifestyle decisions over business decisions. And once again, water brought forth our next big idea.

We rented a houseboat in Amsterdam and got to work brainstorming what our next gathering should look like. We'd gotten some press at the DC10 event that alluded to Summit as "Davos for young businesspeople." Going beyond that called for some serious thinking on how to flip what was now expected of us into something more surreal.

We sat in the cramped living area below deck and gave ourselves permission to blurt out fun, crazy ideas. No matter how far-fetched an idea was, there was always a kernel of insight or something that made us laugh enough to keep going.

We've always believed that one of the most frustrating qualities of big business is the way organizations often crush ideas. When they do, the flame behind their best ideas gets extinguished. The more ideas that get snuffed out, the fewer creative ideas they hear. By design, we didn't have people in our lives saying, "Can you be more realistic?" Besides, you never know when a crazy idea will work.

We'd come to the Netherlands to learn about a company called ID&T that threw large-scale music festivals. With massive productions and elaborate build-outs, ID&T's events transported guests into an intricate dream world. These events filled entire arenas, proving that a little bit of differentiation can go a long way.

We felt that if we constantly pushed ourselves to new, weird, and wild places, it would be only a matter of time before a sparkling idea floated to the surface.

One day, Brett and Jeremy were batting around an idea: "How crazy would it be to charter an entire cruise ship?"

Elliott and Jeff's heads came up at once.

"We're always trying to shoehorn our events into these stodgy hotels," Brett said. "At DC10 we must've spent $50,000 on plants just to make it look like we *weren't* in a hotel. Imagine having the expansive view of the ocean as the backdrop."

That's how Summit at Sea was born.

Brett knew of music events on ships back in his party-throwing days, and Jeremy's band had once been invited to perform at sea back when he was on tour. There were also three-day cruises for a Dave Matthews Band concert and other musical events on ships that were raucous parties and nothing more.

Brett and Jeremy thought this concept was ripe for reinvention. We could create amazing energy with a thousand people connecting in one confined space. Everyone would feel free, surrounded by the open ocean. At the same time, the ship would serve as a container for all that energy, and the energy would build on itself.

A content, music, and art festival at sea? This was very different from booking the Bellagio in Las Vegas or the JW Marriott in Washington, D.C. No matter how good your event is at the Bellagio, you're still doing it in a hotel in a city of hundreds of thousands of people, just like countless other organizations on any given weekend.

What's more, by throwing the event on a cruise ship, everything would be conveniently packaged. With one registration, attendees could purchase their accommodations, meals, and access to programming. It would be a twenty-four-hour-a-day choose-your-own-adventure.

We hopped on our computers to find the cruise company that would be the right fit for the concept. The timing turned out to be perfect. The same ships that leave from Miami in the winter service Europe in the summer, so they were docked in nearby waters. Brett and Jeremy went off to tour one ship in Spain. Elliott and Jeff saw another in Croatia.

We weren't looking for one of those floating cities that could hold five thousand people. But even the smaller ones were still massive. A charter ship that could hold fourteen hundred people—roughly double the number of attendees at DC10—was a sixth of a mile long and fourteen stories high.

We landed on the *Celebrity Century:* an 814-foot ship that we could take over for a three-day trip in April 2011. It'd depart from Miami and stop at a private island in the Bahamas owned by the cruise company. The ship came equipped with 858 crew members, which meant we'd have one crew member for about every two guests. Jeremy and Brett toured the ship while it was docked in the Mediterranean, overwhelmed by the possibilities. The vast pool deck, the portal-tunnel hallways, the upscale restaurants, and the thousand-seat theater would take everything we were creating into new territory. We wanted to transport our attendees into an unexpected world, and we had found it with this ship.

Back on land, we began to engage in conversations with the cruise line's executive team to work out the details and deal points of the charter. Soon we realized that an event of this magnitude brought on new and unanticipated challenges.

The ship would pull into Miami's port only a day before the event started. This meant we'd only have twenty-four hours from the time the ship arrived to load our equipment and build-out materials onto the decks and set up the stages before embarking with fourteen hundred guests.

As we read through the fine print of the contract, we came across another potential issue involving the casino onboard. Cruise deals often ask if you want to participate in the casino proceeds. It could've been an amazing profit center because casinos generally make money, but they don't *always* make money. If the casino lost money, we would've been on the hook to cover the losses. We figured we could donate the profits from the card tables to charity, but there was a risk of it potentially backfiring, leaving us short.

We batted this back and forth for a little while until we realized the decision had already been made for us. There were several professional poker players and card counters

who'd been part of the MIT blackjack team among our potential attendees. Better to steer clear of the casino action.

We continued to talk over the terms and realized we
could use a strategy from the playbook of our first Clinton
event. The cruise company was asking for a nice chunk of
money as a deposit, but it would allow us to pay the rest in
monthly installments leading up to the date of the cruise. We
had just enough to make the deposit, and we figured we
could immediately start to sell tickets for the event to make
the subsequent monthly deposits. That was certainly a great
motivation to sell.

But we quickly discovered that all the successful events
we'd thrown on land had not fully prepared us for sea. When
one of the execs at the cruise company called to ask if our
maritime attorney had any line edits to the contract, we
didn't know how to respond.

"Maritime attorney?"

"Yes, has your maritime attorney reviewed the contract
yet?" he went on. "These ships are governed by international
maritime law. For example, we need to know what your position is on a force majeure."

"Uh, a force ma-what?"

Our questioning seemed to signal to the executive that
we needed more than a little guidance. "Force majeure," he
explained, is the legal term for unforeseeable circumstances
that prevent someone from fulfilling a contract, like a hurri-
cane.

No matter how far we advanced, we always seemed to be
in a new place that left us feeling just as naive as when we
started.

23

LEADERS DON'T HAVE FOLLOWERS; LEADERS CREATE OTHER LEADERS

There was no way we could double the size of our last event and pull off a three-day cruise without hiring people and building a team. We were in the place every business arrives at when it expands.

We'd made a small profit from DC10, which gave us a cushion to do some hiring before our next event. But there was one issue.

We put down a large deposit when we signed the contract with the cruise company, but we hadn't yet started selling tickets to the event. In two short months, we'd gone through our cushion and were once again back to a penny-pinching state as we set out to grow our team.

Many businesses go through this same phase when they're starting out and don't have access to venture capital or the ability to pay talented people who command huge salaries. Culture is always important. But when you're in a tight position, you need to think less about strategy and even *more* about the culture you're assembling.

You're not going to attract traditional candidates who already have well-paying jobs. Instead, you're going to attract those who are thirsty for experiences, are inspired by the same wanderlust, and crave being a part of something bigger than themselves.

We needed to look for people who'd be committed to our community and principles and enticed by the camaraderie that our small team could provide. And we needed to put our (limited) money where our mouths were when it came to everything we had learned about the importance of diversity.

We needed different perspectives, different experiences, different lives. We were seeking inclusion. Inclusion makes you ask: Are these people not only a part of your community but guiding it with you?

When we met the people who were right for our family, we knew almost instantly.

Natalie Spilger, who had participated in our earlier events as an attendee, was a Stanford engineering grad who went on to become a professional soccer player with the Chicago Red Stars. There is a feeling you get around accomplished athletes that is unmistakable. They know how to play on a team. The best athletes play up to the level of their opponents.

For peak athletic performers, in times of crisis or pressure, time slows down, and they excel. It's truly an inspiring quality.

Natalie was smart, funny, creative, and insatiably competitive. What's more, she shared our sense of purpose. She'd started a nonprofit called GreenLaces that presented two simple and powerful steps to help save the planet: One, you needed to make a helpful promise to the planet; two, you needed to wear GreenLaces shoelaces to identify as a fan of the planet. The green laces were a symbol of the environmental green movement, and they were made from recycled plastic.

Natalie was a remarkable creator of physical spaces who could take a small budget and turn it into a big experience. She had a masterly touch for transforming rooms into beautifully designed spaces to create a sense of intimacy and intrigue. She was the first woman to join our team.

We also added Barbara Burchfield, who'd been working with one of Hollywood's biggest directors and running communications at a nonprofit helping Haiti called Artists for Peace and Justice.

And we recruited a gifted young producer out of New York named Audrey Buchanan who, at the time, didn't know if it even made sense to consider working with Summit. Audrey was simultaneously involved with start-ups, nonprofits, and TEDxBrooklyn alongside her day job at one of the country's premier PR firms.

While we were trying to convince Audrey to join us, we invited her to a shark-tagging trip put together by the University of Miami Marine Sciences Department to showcase how to protect the local ecosystem. We often have horrid images of sharks attacking humans swimming near beaches, but the unspoken reality is that humans kill *millions* of sharks every year. This is dangerous to the ecosystem because sharks have an important role in maintaining the species below them in the food chain by culling out the weak and sick. The goal of the trip was to go out to sea to catch, tag, and take blood samples from sharks in order to study and protect them.

When Audrey found herself on top of a massive tiger shark, the expression on her face told us all we needed to know—and the experience told *her* what she needed to know. It was the best recruiting tool we could ever have come up with.

Audrey was in. Over time, she would become our head of content and construct much of Summit's multi-disciplinary approach to live content, fireside chats, and the general way we've gone about the thousand or so talks we've produced as an organization over the years.

These women came in with a high level of professionalism— and expectations. They challenged us in new ways, on everything from how we spoke to how we sent our emails to our forward-facing messaging. They also brought a level of thoughtfulness we just didn't have. After we hosted a talk, we might crow, "That was rad!" There were times we could almost feel them rolling their eyes. "Really?" one would politely inquire. "That was rad? You might want to reconsider how that sounds. It definitely doesn't come off right."

At first, these were hard truths to hear—realities that we often didn't want to acknowledge. But informed critique is the greatest gift you can receive.

Our women team members helped us make our content more relevant and thoughtful. They also sent ripples through other areas of the company and made us realize that we needed to be much more conscious of making sure we said and did what we meant.

These were perhaps the most crucial hires in the Summit story. Without these amazing people, we might've continued to slowly grow the number of women at our events through our relationships, but not nearly to the same degree. And those relationships wouldn't have lasted because our product wouldn't have been representative of what women wanted. Instead of guessing, we now had partners that had an informed strategy.

Within a few months, we had scaled our company to eighteen team members. Our growth felt different from what a more traditional company might experience. It's one thing to work together, but we were determined to *live* together; a tricky dynamic that we would soon have to figure out along the way.

24

LIVE THE BRAND

By this point, the four of us had been living and traveling together for more than ten thousand hours and we were completely in sync with each other's rhythms, habits, and moods. But it's not easy to take a synergy that has developed over several years and scale it when you suddenly add a group of new collaborators.

With eighteen people in our company came a lot of personalities. We knew the strength of Summit was going to be found in keeping the core strong. We needed to be together, even if it meant going back to the same type of bunk-bed living we'd experienced in that tiny New York apartment.

We chose to center the team in Miami to focus on Summit at Sea. We figured we'd rent a few houses, small apartments, and studios around the city and congregate at our office every day. Then one of our team members suggested something that would take us back to our roots and put us all under the same roof.

"The housing market still hasn't fully recovered down here," she said. "There's got to be a big house we could all live in that's on the market for a fraction of the price it would normally get rented."

We decided to run the numbers and soon discovered that if we pooled all of our rent, we could get a house with exponentially more space than if we all rented individually, and at a lower cost per person. This would allow all eighteen of us to chip in just a fraction of what we were currently paying to rent several homes, and we could all live and work in a large, beautiful house. Not only that, but because we wouldn't be paying for office space, the company could put that money toward bringing the rent down for each team member.

Someone else on our team had heard about a sixteen-thousand-square-foot property on Star Island, a community in Biscayne Bay off Miami Beach that's famous for estates owned by P. Diddy, Gloria Estefan, and Shaquille O'Neal. It was a 1980s Mediterranean-style mansion that had been on the market for months and would likely be torn down by the next owner. But at the end of 2010, not many folks were looking to invest in a dilapidated palace on the coast where the sea level was rising. We went to see if the owner would rent it to us while they were looking for a buyer.

Just a couple of us went to view it because we didn't want to let the owner know that eighteen of us were waiting to pile in. We drove through a big sculptural iron gate, which opened automatically and led to a gigantic marble driveway. What followed was just as palatial as the entrance. One part of the house was built to look like a Greek cliffside mansion, with white statues of mythological figures. There were giant gardens, a pool, a Jacuzzi, a badminton court, and a huge deck overlooking the water.

Even though the house was way past its prime, walking through it made us feel like we were in some kind of tropical island fantasy. When we looked at it pragmatically, not only would it double as our office, but the massive space gave us room to build a woodshop and workspace for the fifty to seventy-five production people we foresaw needing during the run-up to Summit at Sea.

The owners agreed to rent it to us. Little did they know that eighteen people would be contributing $1,500 a month to pull it off, while the company picked up the rest.

The home on Star Island introduced a whole new way of living. Nothing we had learned up until that point had shown us how to bring people together into a business commune.

The sleeping arrangements worked themselves out nicely. Some people shared rooms, just like attendees had in the early days of Summit. Most of us were in our mid-twenties, so the dorm lifestyle didn't feel that odd. We set up a trampoline in the back. When tour boats rode by to show off the homes of Rosie O'Donnell and P. Diddy, 150 tourists would snap photos of us working at our outdoor desks or bouncing on the trampoline. They probably wondered why they couldn't place any of our faces in movies they'd seen.

Looking back, though, it was predictable that there would be problems in the kitchen. We were eighteen people coming together without any house rules. Although the rest of the house was enormous, the kitchen was designed with the assumption that only one family would be living there—and one kitchen did not easily accommodate all of us. There was only one refrigerator and one counter to work on. It's hard to point fingers or know exactly where it began, but a few people began to dip into each other's food when they were hungry. The kitchen had started to become a tense place.

Our brand was to bring people together over food, not argue over it, and we needed everybody on our team to be as close as the four of us had become over time. That called for us to reinvent ourselves in a way that allowed everybody in the house to come together in a similar way.

We'd just learned that it made more economic sense to rent one big house instead of individual apartments and studios. Maybe it would be best to centralize food, too.

So we ran the numbers again. We totaled up all the cash and time we were spending buying groceries and going out to eat. Then we analyzed how much it would cost if we had a chef buy the groceries and cook for all eighteen of us a few times a day. We determined that we could make it work at roughly $8 a person for each meal, plus the chef's fee. Add in the time not spent waiting in supermarket lines, cooking sub-par meals, and fighting over who took the last yogurt, and it made total penny-pinching sense.

One member of our team was friendly with a guy who worked at an Italian restaurant in Miami. She thought he might like the opportunity to ditch a thankless kitchen without windows.

His name was Mihai Mosor. He was born in Romania and had migrated to New Jersey. He believed deep in his heart that his entire life was being played out on bonus points, and his gratitude and groundedness were apparent to everyone he met.

He agreed to do a try-out meal for us. We told him we wanted everything to be family-style and healthy, and he blew us away. He cooked up an array of healthy food options and plated it on several serving platters. The vibrant colors and aroma made our jaws drop. We hired him on the spot and asked him if he wanted to move into the house. A week later, he was living and cooking right alongside us.

He was kind, generous—and a third-degree black belt in karate. It was like having an undercover Steven Seagal master chef who had our back. Mihai would walk a mile in the morning to the grocery store—he always insisted on walking—and carried back sacks filled with vegetables and protein. Then he'd prepare big healthy meals of fresh salads, roasted chicken, and grilled veggies—three serving trays containing three different items every day.

When the preparations were complete, Mihai would ring a bell and we'd all descend upon the kitchen simultaneously. Meals were served family-style, we ate family-style, our conversations were family-style, and our relationships became family-style. We got together as a team three times a day and had long-table discussions both on business and on life.

The regular communal meals also helped create a sense of order. Soon there was a schedule on the refrigerator detailing which of us would do the dishes each day. We were in an experimental phase, and it allowed us to discover that the dinner table is the most underrated piece of technology one can have at home—or at an event.

We began inviting people over for meals. We'd interview our guests around the table and ask about their story, how they built their company, or what they were most curious about in their life. We didn't realize it at the time, but we were setting the foundation for what would become the heart of our home, our community, and our brand. We were breaking bread with new friends and old in an intimate and relaxed setting where we could discuss the topics that mattered most to us. It would eventually lead us to an unforgettable day, years down the road, when we'd create a quarter-mile-long table that seated more than nine hundred people, all eating and telling stories side by side.

But a lot of things would have to go right before that day came.

25

BITE OFF MORE THAN YOU CAN CHEW. YOU CAN FIGURE OUT HOW TO CHEW LATER

In the year between DC10 and Summit at Sea, we began to see ourselves more as an art collective than a millennial start-up. "What's your exit strategy?" is one of the most common questions that founders get asked. But in that happy time between May 2010 and May 2011, we realized there was no exit strategy. We didn't want to leave what we'd worked so hard to build. We'd achieved our dream simply by having the freedom to live and create as we pleased, alongside people we cared about. The act of doing was enough. We only wanted to dream bigger and have more impact.

What was the point of selling the company only to hit a payday and lose what we loved doing? Bands sold albums, not their bands. We were in it for the long haul.

Though the four of us had come to the company at different times, we had always seen each other as equals. Brett, Jeff, and Jeremy asked Elliott if he'd be open to sharing the title of co-founder. Elliott liked the idea, and it all became official over a shared meal in our backyard. On top of that,

Elliott felt that Ryan had been instrumental in helping to get Summit off the ground in the beginning, so he called Ryan back in D.C. and offered the co-founder title to him as well, which he graciously accepted. With our partnership solidified, we fanned out in different directions to bring together the pieces we needed to build Summit at Sea.

The four of us often use the phrase "divide and conquer," but not in the way that Julius Caesar executed the strategy in ancient Rome. Instead of employing a strategy to divide our enemies in order to conquer them, the four of us would come together to establish a goal and break it down into parts, and then we'd each go out to conquer a piece.

The first step was putting together a stellar speaker list. We split up and started going to every manner of conference and event, searching for thought leaders we might want to feature.

Elliott was at a gathering in Costa Rica when he ran across Sean Stephenson, who liked to call himself the "Three-Foot Giant." Sean was born with a rare bone disorder called osteogenesis imperfecta that gave him very brittle bones. He described his birth as like being pushed through a bread-making machine, as nearly all of his bones fractured the instant he came into the world. The doctors gave him only twenty-four hours to live. He somehow survived, but for the rest of his life, he could break a collarbone if he sneezed. Sean would live his life in a wheelchair, but he did not let anyone feel sorry for him. Instead, he used his story as the backbone of his mission to rid people of their insecurities. He started as a motivational speaker who mostly talked to schoolkids and church youth groups. But when a young girl asked him why she felt the need to harm herself, he had no answers for her. So he told her he would find them. He went back to school to understand the psychology of self-esteem and became *Dr. Sean Stephenson.*

Sean was up for Summit at Sea.

Just the mention of taking over a ship helped us start conversations that were impossible before. It allowed us to call someone who's difficult to reach and say, "Hey, let me take five minutes to explain why this conference is really worth your time. To start, it's on a ship out in the middle of the ocean."

We knew we needed a big name to anchor the event. We reached out to an entrepreneur who had been an inspiration to all of us: Richard Branson. And by reach out, we mean we made dozens of phone calls and sent even more emails to everyone in our network who we thought might know him. Finally we were able to get through to him. And then, after three months of persistence and follow-up, he said yes and agreed to give a talk.

Jeff and Brett wanted to put us on the map through music. We had yet to have top-tier entertainment. As we pushed ourselves away from being a conference and toward being an interdisciplinary festival, we realized world-class performances were going to be paramount. It was time to step it up from the college-night local DJ bookings of our former lives.

Thanks to a close friend of Summit, Jeff was able to get in touch with The Roots, who had just become the house band for *Late Night with Jimmy Fallon.*

Jeff told The Roots that we were bringing in Richard Branson, going shark-tagging with scientists from the University of Miami, and building a dining experience on a secluded tropical island. They were in. We would need to get all nine band members down to Miami with their equipment the day after they taped a show with Jimmy Fallon and be-

fore the ship set sail. It would be one of the most complicated logistical bookings we'd ever face. But we knew it'd be
worth it.

Meanwhile, Brett worked some of his cold-call magic. He
sent off nearly fifty emails to every established music manager whose contact information could be scrounged up, and
nurtured a friendship that led to a connection with the biggest agent in electronic music.

That agent connected us to Pretty Lights, the face of the
burgeoning American electronic music scene of the late
2000s. Pretty Lights was an appropriate stage name for
Derek Vincent Smith because of the dramatic laser and lighting displays that accompanied his performances. (We'd have
to work out how to do a light show at sea later.) He was so
happy to speak about the future of the music industry that he
agreed to perform for free. Brett also brought in Axwell as a
solo DJ from Swedish House Mafia. Add in Pitbull as an attendee, and we had lifted our game from a local DJ at the JW
Marriott to the kind of talent you would expect to see at a
large-scale music festival.

It might seem odd that Jeremy wasn't highly involved in
this area. But after years on tour with Ice Nine Kills, he
wasn't as enchanted with the booking world as the rest of us.
Instead, he took on one of the most difficult assignments of
his life.

Whenever we'd moved into a new place that had no Wi-Fi
service, Jeremy took it upon himself—as our de facto tech
guy—to hook us up to the Internet. This time, it was Jeremy's
task to make sure that the attendees on the ship had Wi-Fi
while cruising international waters. The ship offered a crude
Internet service that was extremely slow and cost $100 a

person. But we knew that for the people we were bringing in, that just wasn't going to cut it.

This would be no easy fix. But we had just taken over a ship, and nothing seemed too crazy or impossible. So Jeremy came up with the idea to rent satellites in space.

He spoke to a telecom company about buying time on several satellites orbiting around the Earth that could then sync with the ship's system in order to provide high-speed service. Just a few months before, Jeremy had become proficient in putting together our websites and databases. Now he was venturing into the world of NASA-level communications.

Unfortunately, the cost of redirecting a satellite was prohibitive, and soon Jeremy was reaching out to several CTOs in our network to ask for help on finding another solution. They all suggested he build an intranet instead. An intranet is like the Internet except it can be self-contained, which would be ideal for a ship.

This all required installing several servers on the ship, and the complications were endless. We had to hook these servers up to the ship's Internet without compromising the ship's mainframe, which could allow someone to hijack control over the vessel's steering through the Wi-Fi connection (it turned out music wasn't the only thing you could pirate on the Internet).

Jeremy quickly intuited that the task was above his pay grade, so he decided to hire a couple of tech consultants who actually knew what they were doing. They showed up at our home on Star Island and got to work, setting up Wi-Fi routers across the entire yard to simulate how they'd function on the ship.

Fortunately, the system appeared to work, but tensions were still high as one of the biggest concerns from attendees before they bought tickets was the assurance of Internet service. Not only had we guaranteed it, but we'd promised it for free.

Having all four of us going out in different directions and coming back with ideas and successes made us feel like we were moving forward at an exponential rate. Even better, we applied our divide-and-conquer strategy with our growing team so they could fan out to tackle their respective tasks. It was a good thing, because every time we checked one thing off our list, a new task seemed to be added on. Our Star Island garage became the workshop. Soon we had buzz saws, welding machines, and a team working night and day to fabricate tables, a dance floor to fit over the ship's pool, and an assembly line to package up attendee welcome gifts.

We custom-designed a long, curving table for the deck of the cruise ship to serve leafy greens for a hand-tossed salad lunch. It showed up in our driveway in pieces, with none of the bolting functions working properly. For days, Natalie Spilger's younger brother, Nick, sat outside with Michael Hebb—whom we partnered with again to oversee many of our culinary experiences—trying to get this table to work so we could break it down, bring it onto the boat, and quickly reassemble it. A task that should have taken twelve hours took more than four days.

These delays squeezed the timeline on all the other tasks. Hundreds of pillows had to be located for the interior spaces. We needed to find a human-rated crane to lift the sound system onto the stage from the dock. And not only did we have to think about outfitting the ship, but we needed to coordinate an entirely separate elaborate event build-out on the private island that included stages, restaurants, bars, and content zones. A thousand things like this were going on at once, and it soon became abundantly clear that we needed a head of production who could respond to all of them. We recognized ours the instant we met him.

We called our best production lead from DC10, Perry DeCoveny, and began recruiting him to Summit. Perry cut his teeth coordinating dozens of events at once across different cities on New Year's Eve. He was the kind of guy who slept three hours a night during event run-ups and remained calm and unruffled no matter how much stress and chaos swirled around him. Perry came aboard merely four months before the event. He moved into the Miami house and immediately began to negotiate contracts, manage procurement from seventy different vendors, go over insurance policies, handle the temporary contractor staff, and craft the run of show line by line.

Our house on Star Island began to look like a beehive. There was a sense of urgency in the air as we all scurried past the courtyard where a six-by-eight-foot canvas showing the schematics of the ship stood. Floor by floor, it outlined how we were planning to fit in a hundred activities over the course of three days. We were eighteen people without clearly defined roles, helping each other however we could, but at least we were starting to *look* like an actual company.

And come April 7, 2011, we were going to need to *act* like an actual company, in perfect harmony, when we'd have to prepare an event that under normal circumstances would take three days to set up.

We'd have less than twenty-four hours.

26

HONOR THY ERROR AS THE HIDDEN INTENTION

It was a good thing we had no idea we'd be lugging our equipment and furnishings up a Mount Everest of staircases for twenty-four hours—and running into obstacles every step of the way.

We'd thought this would be like loading interior design elements, signage, artwork, and stage decor into a hotel ballroom. It was only after we arrived that we realized checking everything through customs would cause serious delays. The pallets of equipment and staging were sent to the belly of the ship. We'd have to go all the way down near the engine room to find them, then hustle them up fourteen stories to the event spaces spread out over the top decks.

Of course, there were elevators on the *Celebrity Century*. But who had time to wait for them?

Jeremy immediately went to work setting up the intranet. Floor by floor, Jeremy and his team calibrated each Wi-Fi repeater to talk to one another. After some MacGyver-level tinkering, it was time to take the whole system online. They hurried down to their command center, which had been set up in a room the size of a broom closet, and powered the servers on, their stomachs tightening as the lights on the system began to flash one by one.

With the servers humming, Jeremy jumped on his phone to test the app. It worked. It actually worked! It was an invisible behind-the-scenes piece of mastery that the attendees would never know about, and one of those moments that only we could celebrate. We tend to remember only the things that go wrong. When we do things right, it's the sound of silence that should be celebrated.

Twenty-four hours after we'd begun bringing equipment aboard, we were still testing the lights, setting up signs, and building out event spaces. But it was time for the passengers to start boarding. Our team had been dreaming of this moment for over four months now. Jeremy and a member of our team went to the top deck and proudly unfurled a 120-by-80-foot banner over the side of the ship that read:

MAKE NO SMALL PLANS

It felt to Jeremy like he was planting a flag on the moon. It was a beautiful sight, except for one problem: Most of our guests weren't on hand to see it.

One lesson we learned that morning was that it doesn't matter how prepared you are, because the day will never unfold the way you planned it. What matters most is how you react to the unexpected moments.

We'd asked attendees to board at 9 A.M., but we didn't anticipate that our guests wouldn't follow instructions. We had told everyone it was important to arrive early to start the boarding process, as there were forms to be filled out and passports to be inspected. It was like the TSA checkpoints at an airport, but much more time-consuming.

Maybe our guests had decided to take meetings that morning. Maybe they'd slept in. Maybe they were at brunch, or just landed and were heading straight from the airport. We had no idea. All we knew was that very few people showed up to board on time. By high noon, only a few guests had trickled in. Finally, at three in the afternoon, a massive block of attendees began to stream into the port, creating a huge bottleneck, and a line that snaked down the pier.

The event hadn't even started, and our guests were beginning to grumble. We rushed to the port to greet everyone and show our appreciation, but found the majority of our attendees—including many of our heroes—universally pissed after learning it would be more than a two-hour wait to board the ship.

One attendee looked Elliott in the eye and sarcastically said: "Is this a joke? I've never waited in a line this long in my life. Nice event you're putting on here."

We quickly asked one of our DJs to set up in the hallway of the port building, hoping the music would help ease the tension. We then radioed our culinary team and got them to deliver us cut fruit and beverages. We placed them on trays and moved down the line, serving everyone, connecting eye to eye and greeting each guest. More importantly, we introduced hundreds of people to one another before they even boarded. As soon as attendees started connecting with others in the queue, that summer-camp feeling we had always strived for washed over the dock and made everybody happy in a way they hadn't expected. They may have been stuck in line, but they were free to be in the moment. As it turned out, the party started before they even set foot on the ship.

Once attendees cleared the maritime equivalent of customs, each was given a keycard that granted access to certain parts of the ship. But as the long line moved forward, we got word that a few people had gotten caught trying to crash the event. Someone who had successfully boarded stepped off the boat and passed along a keycard to someone who hadn't registered to attend.

The crashers saw it comically, as though they'd hopped a fence to get into a music festival. But U.S. Customs and Border Protection saw it seriously, as though they'd sneaked onto an airplane.

Elliott arrived just as the gatecrashers were getting cuffed. "None of this needs to happen!" he said to the CBP agents. "It's okay by us—you can just let them go."

"You need to keep your mouth shut and take three steps back," one of the agents shot back, "or you're going to jail, too."

Elliott had no time to argue. We were getting frantic messages from guests who'd left their passports at home and wanted to know what to do. On top of that, we got word that The Roots might not make it in time after getting delayed following their taping of Jimmy Fallon's show.

Our tensions eased a little when we looked around and saw who *was* on the boat: Richard Branson, Chris Anderson (the chief curator of TED), and Beth Comstock (then the vice chair at General Electric). We waited, waited, and waited. Then, moments before the ship had to depart, The Roots stepped aboard.

As the sun set, the four of us stood on the second story

above the pool, scanning the ocean and the skyline of Miami. We heard a deep, rumbling foghorn—that ceremonial sound that blows on every ship when it departs—and we felt that symbolic lurch as we pulled away from shore.

We couldn't believe it. We'd done it. It all worked. It actually *worked*!

Then, five minutes later, the intranet didn't.

People immediately noticed. *How am I going to stay in touch with my team? How am I going to stay on top of the deal I was working on?* Or, much more importantly: *How am I going to communicate with my family back home?*

The attendees started to become agitated, wandering around the deck holding their phones in the air like a telecom commercial. Those who weren't looking for a signal were running to our team, who, in turn, were all running to Jeremy, asking him what the hell had happened.

Jeremy jumped into action, frantically trying to figure out a solution. But as we moved away from the port and out into the sea, we soon hit a point of clear defeat. We had hit the Internet iceberg only a few miles offshore.

Then something unfolded that none of us could've expected. Attendees began to approach us to say how great it was that the Internet *wasn't* working. They realized how much their phones distracted them from real human connection, and they loved that they could be fully present, surrounded by strangers who were quickly becoming friends.

It was a great lesson for us: Honor thy error as an act of hidden intention.

What had at first seemed like a failure and a fiasco became a core piece of our culture going forward. We had a new motto: *There's no Wi-Fi where we're going, but we promise you'll find a better connection.*

27

IT ONLY HAS TO HAPPEN ONCE
TO BE REMEMBERED

The opening speaker at Summit at Sea is no longer with us, but he will never be forgotten by anyone who was aboard that ship.

Dr. Sean Stephenson rolled himself out onto the stage in his wheelchair, his hands pumping the souped-up rims. Sean wanted to use his disability to rid the world of its insecurities, and at Summit at Sea, he made his point before uttering a word. In a T-shirt and jeans, he couldn't have been more relaxed. The way he artfully pivoted around the stage in his wheelchair was a clear sign he'd learned to take complete control over the "container" he was born in. His smile told everyone that his physical body had no control over his self-esteem.

"I have some good news, and I have some bad news," Sean began. "We'll start with the bad news. The bad news is that several people have already been taken off the boat. The good news is they were the only ugly ones."

The room erupted in uncomfortable laughter. People

looked around at each other shyly before looking back to the man on stage—at the person who had spent his entire life with people avoiding eye contact with him.

"You made the cut," Sean continued. "So you can stop worrying when you're out in your bathing suit at the pool."

He relished another comedic pause.

"That's my self-esteem talk."

For twenty minutes, with line after line, Sean stripped the ego out of an auditorium full of overachievers: "Confidence is about *improving* ourselves. Arrogance is about *proving*." "Emotion is the currency of humanity. And the individuals that are truly able to understand how to reach the masses emotionally are the wealthiest people on the planet." "The best way to get love is to give love."

He conducted exercises like asking the audience—people he'd only met a few hours earlier—to greet the people sitting beside them like arrogant assholes. He then asked them to greet each other like extremely shy people. Everyone observed how the different exercises made them shut down or become standoffish to those around them. Then he instructed us all to greet each other like long-lost friends. The room erupted in hugs, high-fives, smiles, and high energy. When Sean closed his talk, every single person in the auditorium felt a connection.

He passed away eight years later at the age of forty, a full thirty-nine years later than what doctors had predicted when he was born. His time at Summit at Sea will permeate our lives and Summit's culture forever. That's because of the lessons Sean instilled in us: Who we are is not a reflection of how we look. We are a collection of our actions, not our appearances. And by welcoming fellow humans with open arms and enthusiasm, we can connect to something so much deeper and more meaningful within ourselves and with each other.

When Sean rolled onto the stage, he *set* the stage. After that, the entire event was like an explosion of serendipity wherever you turned.

In one hallway, a dense circle formed around serial entrepreneur Gary Vaynerchuk, with people throwing out questions and getting into debates that lasted *six hours*. Watching GaryVee was like seeing a chess grandmaster playing multiple games at once, moving from board to board, and it backed up what Jeff had observed at the White House years earlier: People loved learning and gathering in the corridor.

At the time, it wasn't common for folks in entertainment, tech, impact, and investment to interact deeply with one another. But here wires were crossing in a way they'd never crossed before. Summit at Sea was where PayPal co-founder Peter Thiel met and funded Chester Ng and Jack Abraham, who would go on to create Atomic, one of Silicon Valley's preeminent venture studios and incubators. M. Sanjayan, the lead scientist at the Nature Conservancy, spoke on the importance of no-take zones in the ocean, to allow the ecosystem to recover and thrive. Over the course of three days, we helped him to raise $1 million to create a seventy-square-mile marine protected area in the Bahamas.

Anybody could walk up to Tony Hsieh from Zappos and start a comfortable conversation. There were heroes for young female entrepreneurs, like Crowdrise co-founder Shauna Robertson and Acumen Fund founder Jacqueline Novogratz. Pitbull and Questlove directed a band of attendees in an interior stairwell using instruments from the music jam room.

The speakers' messages were deeply relevant to the entire ship. Peter Diamandis, who established the XPRIZE Foundation, spoke on the ability for us to change the world through rapidly evolving technologies. Beth Comstock, of General Electric, painted a clear picture of how technological innovation was now the domain of start-ups, not the GEs of the world. She had a great quote: "The pace of change will never be slower than it is today." M. Sanjayan pushed us to think deeply about how we were degrading our planet—as well as our personal potential to be part of the solutions. Every speech, every corridor, every meal, and every elevator brought people together.

Late into the evening, Brett looked up at the lasers during the performance by Pretty Lights and watched as dancers on deck fell into the pool in revelry. Jeremy kept getting congratulated by everyone who was grateful that the ship had no Internet service: *What a genius concept to force everyone to live in the present moment for the next three days. How did you come up with the idea?*

There were times when it seemed that the ship could no longer hold the event's energy—literally. The audio and lighting systems were pulling so much energy from the engine room at one point during The Roots' show that it overloaded the engine room and caused a blackout on board.

But the band just kept on playing acoustically on their drums, horns, and saxophones, and led the crowd through a once-in-a-lifetime unplugged performance.

Summit at Sea was not the result of excellence that had been compiled through years of experience. In fact, we're sure we looked like amateurs to the co-founder of Lollapalooza when the lights went out in the middle of the concert. (He told us so afterward, and we greatly appreciated the feedback.) But Lollapalooza had been doing it for two decades by this point, and you can't compare your Chapter 1 to someone else's Chapter 27. The experience of Summit at Sea was, in essence, the energy and vibrations bouncing off the clean lines of the ship's hull and out into the ocean.

On the third day, we anchored and turned off the engines a mile from the island where we had programming and a culinary feast prepared. Shortly thereafter, seven attendees jumped overboard from the seventh story of the ship.

Jeff had just finished one of the most high-minded conversations he'd ever been part of—between Sir Ronald Cohen, the man who invented the social-impact bond, and the street artist JR—when he heard the boat's emergency alarm.

Mayday! Mayday!

We rushed over to starboard to make sure everyone who'd jumped was okay—and they were, thankfully. But the authorities on the ship did not view it as an impulsive prank led by a few professional extreme athletes. They wanted to put every attendee who'd jumped overboard into a holding pen and then turn them over to the authorities on land for violation of some international maritime law. It took every ounce of bargaining power we had to keep them out of the brig.

It was seventy-two hours of nonstop moments like this. Elliott was playing emcee for most of this time. On the final day, as he was about to introduce one of the highest-profile speakers to more than a thousand people in the auditorium, the speaker told him he couldn't go on.

"What do you mean you can't go on?"

"I left my lucky bracelet back in the room."

"That's okay. When you go back to the room it'll be there."

"But I won't be able to get into the flow on stage without it."

Meanwhile, a backstage announcement was telling everyone to prepare to go on. "Dim the house lights . . ."

Elliott grabbed the speaker's room key and sprinted a quarter mile to the other end of the boat, raced up seven flights of stairs, got into the speaker's room, rummaged through all the speaker's belongings until the bracelet appeared, then sprinted with it down seven stories and a quarter mile back to the auditorium. Elliott passed over the bracelet and took the mic to introduce the speaker, not realizing that he was sweating through his shirt and panting like an overheated dog.

Everybody on the ship was pushed as far as they possibly could go, and after seventy-two hours, it showed. As we performed our closing talk in the main auditorium to bid farewell to the attendees, our entire team of eighteen came up onto the stage and sat in chairs strung from end to end. But as we said our thank-yous, one staff member literally fell asleep onstage and tipped over onto the person seated next to him. There was simply nothing more anyone could give.

We wanted to get the most out of every moment, and the four of us didn't get any sleep on the final night. We were bleary-eyed and barely able to stand as everyone began to disembark on that final morning. It was particularly meaningful to us to look each and every guest in the eye and thank them for coming. After everything that followed the insensitive email we'd sent out to sell our Aspen event just three years earlier, it gave us the sense of closure that we needed.

And, as always, a moment of closure for us meant the start of something much bigger.

28

CHANGE YOUR POINT OF VIEW TO CHANGE YOUR POINT OF VIEW

The only problem with throwing an epic gathering on a cruise ship is that it's nearly impossible to top. It was the biggest idea we'd ever come up with, and we couldn't think of anything more grandiose. Our community knew we could go big and go hard—and now they were going to expect each event to top the last.

But as exciting as having 1,400 people on a cruise liner was, we knew from feedback that our community wanted things to feel more intimate again. It's one thing to grow from 125 to 250, and it's another to grow from 250 to 750. But when you grow from 750 to 1,400 in one leap, that's something else entirely. It would be difficult to continue to scale like that and maintain the core of what we started.

We had a long debate about it. We had never heard of a festival or conference making its next event *smaller*. The whole purpose of an events business is to scale. From a financial perspective, it didn't make any sense to shrink our gatherings—but from a community point of view, it did. We thought back to that night in Washington, D.C., when Tony Hsieh took us aside to stress the importance of culture when building community. When we looked at it that way, it made sense to focus on ROC (return on community) over ROI (return on investment). Instead of maximizing profits, we'd focus on building trust from our attendees for decades to come.

So we scaled back our next event to eight hundred people and started a tradition of going from sea to ski by booking it at Squaw Valley (now known as Palisades Tahoe) in Lake Tahoe. We called it Basecamp. By this stage, tickets were basically selling themselves, and by halving the number of attendees, we could use the extra time to improve the programming and experiences we wanted to create for our guests in an intimate winter wonderland.

There was one problem. Miami was a long way from the Sierra Nevadas. Now that we didn't need to be in South Beach, we realized it might be time to replicate the Star Island experience on the West Coast. We decided to pick up and move the entire team to Los Angeles. This would put us close to Hollywood, and it was also a stone's throw from the tech entrepreneurs in Silicon Valley.

One of our team members, David Denberg, had grown up in Malibu, and he connected us to a real estate agent to handle our unusual request: "We need a furnished eighteen-bedroom house on the beach."

It was a lot of money, but it would be less than we had been spending in Miami. The rental price came out to about $1,000 a month per person, with the company covering a portion of the cost in lieu of office space. Once again, it was far cheaper than if we'd each rented our own apartment.

There was *one* home available that met our specs: a large

house perched on the Malibu coastline an hour outside of Los Angeles. Because it had been built before 1977, it predated and therefore was exempt from the California Coastal Commission maximums for single-family square footage. That allowed it to be much larger than homes now built on the coastline. None of us could take a tour from twenty-seven hundred miles away, so we looked at photos instead.

The grounds appeared majestic on the outside, but the inside revealed 1970s orange carpet and antiquated wallpaper. Paint appeared to be chipping off all the door frames, and the windows all seemed to have a thick film on them. It was, however, the only place big enough to house us all. So we figured, no big deal—we'd just apply some of our newfound space-making skills and clean the place up. We signed a lease to move in June 1, 2011, sight unseen.

After Summit at Sea, the entire team took off the rest of the month of May to travel and recuperate. We all made our own plans to fly into California and make our way to the beach house at the start of summer. The first time the four of us drove the hour north of L.A. to see what we'd gotten ourselves into, we missed the house entirely. The entry was totally hidden from the street. We only realized it after the addresses of subsequent homes told us that we'd gone too far. Once we finally found the driveway, there were overgrown hedges and an unkempt terraced garden that showcased hundreds of roses of all colors, leading down to a large brick home covered with ivy. Huge elegant double doors opened into a foyer with a view of the Pacific Ocean that went on for miles.

We toured the grounds, nodding.

"This will do."

"That kitchen will definitely work."

"Okay, this view is insane!"

But there was no electricity, and we had to run an extension cord to a neighbor's home for a few days to get power. Soon we were moving around all the furniture, setting up one room as a command center and another as an ashram-like sanctuary. There was a wide variety of bedrooms, ranging from ones that had a highly desirable balcony view of the ocean to windowless ones in the basement. So we priced every room accordingly, and, based on seniority, had each team member choose accommodations that suited their budget.

Everybody began to settle in. Cardboard boxes and half-opened suitcases littered the halls, and a sense of excitement filled the cavernous space. Then, in the middle of our first night, we heard someone shrieking. One of our team members who'd chosen to convert the library into a bedroom was screaming so loudly she woke up everyone in the house and sent us scurrying into the foyer.

"There's a man in my room!" she bellowed, terrified. "I mean, a ghost. A man-ghost. This house is haunted!"

We tried to calm her down. Of course there wasn't a ghost in the house, we told her. Or a man. This place was impossible for us to find, and we were *looking* for it. How would an unknown intruder find his way here and get inside?

"No," she said, "he was standing in the window. I woke up and he was right there."

One of our team members, a former football player at the University of Colorado, rolled his eyes. He muttered that it was all absurd, and volunteered to scour the room for her. He found nothing. Eventually everyone relaxed and returned to their rooms—except, of course, that one team member. There was no way she was going to sleep in the library that night, and she opted for the couch in the living room.

A few days later, when our former football player was upstairs by himself, he started howling.

"Oh, my God! *There's the man!*"

That was the last time the mysterious visitor was spotted. If there was in fact a ghost at all, he was friendly—and he was a great reminder that sometimes there are unexplainable moments that challenge our perception of reality. This fueled us to want to create even more perspective-shifting moments at our events. The ghost also turned out to be a great conversation starter at the communal meals we began hosting at the house.

Basecamp was still six months away, but we realized we didn't have to wait to create a deeper sense of community. We could do so immediately, in our new home. When we reflected on the long-table dinners we'd hosted on Star Island, it was clear to see that deep bonds had formed among our small team and a few guests. What if we could multiply that magic with a hundred guests at our new beach house? And what if we held these meals twice a week?

We knew the excitement this would bring to our team. However, we had no idea of the impact it would make on the guests we'd bring together and the ripples it would send far and wide. We'd soon discover that these dinners would be the greatest engine for relationship development we'd ever uncovered.

29

THE ART OF SOCIAL SCULPTURE

If you had asked our chef, Mihai, if our time at the Malibu home was a period of scaling back, he might have looked at you as if you were crazy—especially if you had asked him on a Tuesday or Thursday night. Mihai had been accustomed to cooking for twenty people in Miami. But on Tuesdays and Thursdays in Malibu, he was preparing dinners for a hundred.

The dinner table became our focus, and we turned to our friend Michael Hebb for help. Michael was famous for throwing dinner parties in unique locations and with unique themes—like the median of an interstate highway in Oregon, or a dinner for strangers he met on the street over the course of one day. He used food to experiment with art and human connection, and he specialized in developing conversations around the table. Culture, he said, had been shaped by the table throughout history.

When we first asked Michael if he would come to help us host a dinner, we told him we could set up a big table in our living room. He told us that our idea wasn't going to work. Instead, he'd come by in the afternoon and we'd all build the table together. We didn't quite understand what he was up to at first, but he'd never let us down in the past, so we trusted him implicitly. When he arrived, he walked outside onto a huge upstairs balcony with stunning sea views.

"Here's what we're going to do," he told our assembled team. "I want everyone to find all the coffee tables in the house and carry them to the balcony. Next, I want you to get all the cushions and pillows from the couches, carry them here, and we'll use them as seats under the coffee tables. Then I want you to bring twelve lamps and extension cords. We're going to turn all the lights off in the entire house except for these lamps."

Several hours later, once the meal was prepared and our guests had arrived, there we were, sitting outside on cushions at nine o'clock at night, overlooking the ocean. We listened to the crashing waves, our faces lit only by lamps. Michael taught us how to see not what a space *was* but what it *could* be. From that moment on, we never accepted a space as static. We understood that anything could be transformed into whatever we wanted it to be.

We also recalibrated how we invited guests to dinner. We didn't start by thinking, "We haven't seen so-and-so for a while. Let's invite them." Instead, we organized each meal around a theme to answer the question of why we were throwing this dinner. To meet people? To spend time with friends? To give back to the community? To address a certain topic of conversation?

The motivation we chose determined the people we'd invite. We knew that the more diverse the attendees, the more complex the conversation, and the better the experience. We became as intentional with our invitations as we were with the meal itself.

Guests got a personalized invitation to visit our home for dinner. Depending on the evening, we'd have actors, tech leaders, environmentalists, angel investors, scientists, artists, and musicians—most importantly, kind and caring people—gathered around our table. Because we kept these parties off the radar, nobody had any idea who was coming when they walked in—they had to trust us in our promise to convene people they'd like to meet. We used narrative and ritual to create experiences that never could've happened in a restaurant, and we served food family-style.

Normally, for this type of meal, you'd have an executive chef and two or three helpers in the kitchen, a serving crew, and a cleaning crew. We had Mihai, and that was it. He operated like a machine, churning out breakfast and lunch for our team, and then turning his attention to preparing the evening's menu. To this day, we are still in awe of the number of delicious meals he was able to serve up out of that kitchen.

Every Tuesday and Thursday we brought the food out on huge trays ourselves and served it on a long table. There were no serving dishes, nor did any of us walk around like a general manager of a four-star restaurant asking, "How was your dinner tonight?" We made everyone feel like they were in their own home, like they could open the refrigerator and reach for the milk carton. We called it "barefoot hospitality."

Though every evening was different, one thing we'd always ask was for an attendee to make an opening toast. We'd often call upon someone without tipping them off to keep it vulnerable and real. We'd ask them to tell the group about an incredible project they were working on, and you never knew what might come up. It might have been Leslie Odom Jr., a star of *Hamilton,* singing to us four years before he and the show arrived on Broadway. Or it might have been an evolutionary biologist explaining to us what they found so exciting about biomimicry.

At the close of dinner, everyone would clean up. Even this became a communal experience.

"Before everybody leaves the table," we'd say, "we need everyone to put your left hand in the air."

All the left hands would shoot up.

"Now, put your right hand in the air."

People would be wondering what was going on as they raised their right hand.

"Now, bring them down onto the table!"

A solid thud would resound around the room, followed by light laughter.

"This is called the box. Everything inside your box is your responsibility. If you could help us clean up by bringing the things within your box to the sink, we'd really appreciate it."

And just like that, people who would normally be waited on at a restaurant were taking their own dirty dishes to our sink.

We honed the format and natural flow of the evening week after week. Eventually, we took the barefoot hospitality concept with us wherever we went. Anytime we traveled to a new city, we coordinated the same type of dining experience we'd been doing back in Malibu.

Some of these meals became once-in-a-lifetime experiences, like the time Thom Yorke, the lead singer of Radiohead, showed up at a dinner we threw in a friend's apartment in New York City. At a certain point, Thom excused himself to use the restroom. As he was returning to the table, he stumbled upon a piano in a back room. He sat down and began to play. Not for an audience, not for us, just for himself.

A few minutes later, another guest looking for the bathroom heard the piano and stumbled into the back room. There was Thom Yorke, playing the piano and softly singing. The guest froze in the hallway and could barely contain himself as he texted other guests who were still at the table.

One by one we left the table. After a while, some forty people were crammed into the room, listening to one of the most intimate concerts of their lives.

Whispers of these experiences, and talk of our dinners in Malibu and what we'd pulled off at Summit at Sea, began to ripple outward. More and more people became curious about what we were doing and began reaching out to us. One of them was a young woman who headed up the coast to find us at our home.

Her name was Shira Abramowitz, and she was about to graduate from McGill University in Montreal. Shira had helped start an environmentally friendly business to reduce waste at her school.

She became intrigued with the concept of social entrepreneurship and started to look at like-minded companies. After some digging, she found our address in Malibu. A friend of hers drove her up the Pacific Coast Highway and left her outside a gate that she thought led to our home. As she stepped through, the gate closed on her and locked her in. Only then did she realize that the house wasn't ours.

Eventually she found the right house, and we were lucky she did. It was a turning point for us. We'd spent years constantly searching for people to come to our events, but *she* found *us*. We took her up on her proposal to work with us, and she's helped lead our programming, content, and impact work ever since.

She found a home within our team. That was a new concept to us: home. We'd been nomads ever since we'd come together and flown off with our single suitcases. But our time in Malibu was teaching us the importance of a sense of place, and we began to wonder if we could find a permanent place to call our own.

30

SPACESHIPS DON'T COME EQUIPPED WITH REAR-VIEW MIRRORS

Many times, you schedule an introductory meeting over a cup of coffee and nothing much comes out of it. It's friendly, and you move on to the next. But you have to keep taking those meetings to ensure you don't miss the one that could change everything.

Such a meeting occurred when Elliott left our Malibu home for Los Angeles on a Saturday morning in August 2011. He was meeting a venture capitalist who had attended Summit at Sea, Greg Mauro. Greg was building a tech start-up and investing in education companies, but he'd reached out because he was curious about the Summit community. The meeting was supposed to last an hour, but it went on for eight.

Elliott had long observed that many people you meet for coffee are more interested in talking about themselves than learning about you. Not Greg. He wanted to answer the same question we had been thinking about: What more could the Summit community be?

The four of us had been discussing this nonstop since we'd moved to Malibu. Up until Summit at Sea, our long-term vision had been to create once-in-a-lifetime experiences through events. But we noticed that members of our community were meeting up to maintain their friendships in between our events. We sensed that we needed a way to connect our community for more than just one long weekend a year.

The energy from our Tuesday and Thursday night dinners in Malibu was a call to action. Those meals showed us that we needed to do something to continue the momentum of our gatherings. We needed a sense of permanence—not just a rented beach house, but something that felt like home.

What that "home" actually looked like, we had no idea. It wasn't like we were sitting around mapping out a plan to buy a farm and turn it into our own retreat space. We didn't exactly know what we wanted. But that same question kept echoing in our minds: *What more could Summit be?*

As Elliott and Greg sipped their coffee, Greg pointed out that entrepreneurs and angel investors in San Francisco often took meetings at Starbucks because they didn't know where else to go. He thought it would be smart to set up a club where the entire Summit community could get together on a regular basis, and he even had an option on a building in San Francisco that he sensed might be a good fit.

Elliott and Greg spent the day driving around L.A. looking at similar spaces and brainstorming ideas for how such a club might come alive. After so much time traveling the world, Elliott was excited about the idea of Summit having a place where it could finally grow roots. Along the way, Elliott asked Greg where he lived.

Greg mentioned that he'd spent his winters during the last five years in a small town in Utah called Eden.

"Why Eden?" Elliott asked.

Greg explained that he and a friend had researched the twenty-five best ski towns in America, narrowed it down to the best five, and then decided that Eden was the hidden gem. Their favorite ski resort in North America, Powder Mountain, was in Eden, and Greg had bought a house close to the resort. It was about an hour from Salt Lake City International Airport, so it was quick to get to the mountains no matter where Greg was in the world. Most people who flew into that airport for ski trips drove forty-five minutes to resorts such as Park City, Alta, Snowbird, Deer Valley, Solitude, or Brighton, which are all east of Salt Lake City. But if you drove north for an hour instead, you'd arrive at Powder Mountain. There, far fewer skiers enjoyed an uncrowded ski resort in a picturesque lakeside mountain town with no stoplights. It was a secluded heaven.

Not only that, Greg continued, but the whole Powder Mountain Resort was for sale . . . and he had an interest in buying it.

Elliott returned to Malibu and told the rest of us about his day with Greg: how angel investors were meeting at coffee shops, and how that might present an opening for some sort of Summit club in San Francisco.

We weren't in the habit of denying ideas just because they were difficult, but we honestly weren't that interested in moving to San Francisco or creating a permanent experience in an already crowded city.

"You open a space in a city and you're a hot ticket for a year or two," Brett said, "but it's an operational headache, and over time, everybody forgets about your amazing space."

We agreed that, for us, there was very little longevity in the city club idea. As we talked it through, we decided we wanted a place where our community could grow over time, not just a place to have lunch meetings. We wanted a place where people could bring their kids and families—a place that would have a future.

"Well," Elliott said, "there was this other project that Greg mentioned. He's got a home in Utah at apparently one of the best and largest ski resorts in the country. I guess the whole resort is for sale."

"What's this mountain called?" Jeremy asked.

"I think it's called Powder Mountain."

Brett's eyes lifted. "Powder Mountain?"

Jeremy's did, too. "*The* Powder Mountain?"

Back when Brett was a college freshman, he had flown to Colorado to meet Jeremy for a ski trip. He'd heard the skiing out west was much better than on the East Coast, and he was curious to check it out. On his flight, he got into a conversation with the person next to him about skiing in the Rockies.

"If you *really* want to ski out west, you need to look outside of the Rockies," the woman said. "You need to learn about Powder Mountain."

Brett had vowed to check it out, but the opportunity never arose.

"How soon can we see it?" Jeremy asked.

We were intrigued. We had no idea what opportunities and potential the mountain held, nor the mess we were about to get ourselves into. What we did know was that there was only so much we could build into the floor of an office building in downtown San Francisco. Deep in nature on a mountain range, the possibilities were endless.

If you get a chance meeting and it leads to something

you're intrigued by, you've got to pursue that path and lean into it. We've always believed that. Once the search is in process, something will be found.

We had no idea if Powder Mountain was actually for sale. Or how much a mountain costs. But we were all in to follow our gut feeling.

"What's the worst thing that could happen?" we asked.

As it turned out, a lot.

31

WHEN YOU HAVE THE RIGHT OPPORTUNITY, IT'S ALWAYS THE RIGHT TIME

We jumped on a plane thirty-six hours later. Greg picked us up at the airport in Salt Lake City and gave us a quick download during the drive to Powder Mountain.

"Eden is one of the last great open spaces in the western United States," he said. "It's as off the grid as you could possibly get and yet only an hour from an international airport."

The resort, Greg explained, had been started by a colorful local character named Alvin Cobabe, who had entered medical school when he was in his forties and graduated as the oldest person in Utah to become a certified doctor at that time. Alvin came from a family of sheepherders who owned the land that would become Powder Mountain. As he added acreage over time, he built a road and a double-chair ski lift for the community.

That was back in 1972. Cobabe kept the site quaint and magical. A small ski school was erected and an outdoor barbecue was installed. Cobabe's whole philosophy was summed up in a quote that was placed on the side of a Powder Mountain building: "You're only a stranger once."

Cobabe maintained the mountain that way for more than thirty years before his family sold it in 2006. He lived to be ninety-nine years old, and before he died in 2017, he saw the land change hands two more times.

As we learned, Powder Mountain was in the hands of a private equity firm that had announced plans to build nearly three thousand large houses, put in new high-speed ski lifts, and install an eighteen-hole golf course. The town's six hundred residents were furious. They filed suit to stop the development in a case that had worked its way to the Utah Supreme Court. The residents were committed to protecting their backyard gem. We hadn't even arrived yet, but we were already in support of the local community's values.

Greg headed toward the town center.

"Welcome to the four-way stop," he said. "Eden's downtown." We smiled at the irony. On the right we saw empty farmland and used farm equipment. On the left sat a grocery store and a gas station. As we pressed on, we passed farm after farm until we reached the foot of Powder Mountain.

Suddenly, it felt like we were entering a national park. Thousands of aspen trees crawled up the mountains on both sides of us. A rushing creek with crystal clear water flowed past the right side of the car windows as we snaked up a meandering road to the top.

"One of the things that makes this place unique," Greg said, "is that Powder Mountain has an inverted topography: It flattens out at the top. At most mountains, there are aggressive peaks and you take a lift to the summit, so you're forced to build all the homes at the base of the mountain.

Here, you can drive to the top and ski down. Then the chair-lifts bring you back up. So you could build on the *top* of the mountain with amazing panoramic views you can't get any-where else."

The paved road ended abruptly, leaving a raw dirt road ahead of it. As we approached the top, we came to a steel cable hanging across the road with a sign on it: CLOSED APRIL 15—DECEMBER 1.

We all looked at Greg, wondering if he had some sort of plan.

"No cars are allowed, but they can't keep us from walking around," he said. "A lot of people like to come up here for the sunset. We can just park and walk up."

We stepped out of the car and ducked under the cable. We took in the pristine air, and after about a hundred feet, we were stunned by the great reveal.

In an instant, we could see the full expanse of the snow-capped mountains around us in all directions, out past Utah to Wyoming, Idaho, and even over the Great Salt Lake to Ne-vada. We looked down at the valley of Eden below, sur-rounded by rolling hills and upward-reaching peaks.

"Have you ever seen anything this beautiful?" Greg asked.

We were too overwhelmed to answer.

It looked like someone had taken a photo of Switzerland and brought it to life in front of our eyes. *How had we barely even heard of this place?* we wondered. *And why would anyone give up such a majestic paradise? Finally, how much did this paradise cost?*

Greg assured us he'd find the owner and get the asking price.

We spent the rest of the day venturing around the mountain and strolling through the small town center of Eden, dreaming of what we could create in this magical setting.

There is no better way to be introduced to a place than by having the right guide. We had never explored a project even close to this scale, and Greg seemed to fit with a mindset we all embraced: Replace your weaknesses with a partner's strengths. We were wandering creatives, community builders, and experts in hospitality by this point. Greg understood finance in a much deeper way than we did. We leaned toward the right side of the brain; he leaned toward the left. Our skill sets complemented each other.

The next morning, we hopped a flight back to Los Angeles, buzzing with excitement. In the days and weeks that followed, all we could think about was Powder Mountain. It was hard to keep it a secret, but we did the best we could so that our team could keep its focus on Basecamp. By late September, the event was only four months away, and we trusted our team to book the final speakers, build out the run of show, and plan the finishing touches. We were so fortunate to have a competent organization that stepped up, which allowed the four of us to spend as much time as we could calling land developers, studying master plans from other developments, and gaining rudimentary knowledge of water rights and zoning laws. In the evenings, we'd come together to share what we'd learned that day, then talk late into the night about what we could do on Powder Mountain.

We discovered a common trend among ski resorts—a trend that didn't resonate with any of us, and one that we were determined to buck.

Brett was the first to catch on to it. He'd recognized it as a teenager, but it had never been relevant to him until now.

When Brett was in junior high school, a man named Les Otten was the CEO of the American Skiing Company, and he began buying the resorts that Brett loved in Vermont, New Hampshire, and Maine. Otten took the company public and used the proceeds to build a theme-park atmosphere that crammed in as many lifts and units as possible to attract massive crowds. This made Otten a multimillionaire. While Brett respected Otten's business acumen, he didn't like what was happening to the skiing experience at his favorite resorts. It felt more and more diluted.

But the trend didn't stop there. The same tactics were being used all across America. By the 2010s, three huge companies controlled most of the ski resorts with the same mass-market management. We learned that the current residents of Eden were terrified that their beloved mountain was going to turn into Disneyland. Maybe, we thought, the people of Eden would get behind a new vision. We were attracted to the place for the same reasons they were, and we wanted to protect it just as ferociously.

We nailed a massive whiteboard to Brett's bedroom wall and began sketching out ideas for a completely new approach. What could a mountain resort of the future look like? We wanted to limit development—and unlike the private-equity firm, we wanted the homes to be small and eco-friendly. Instead of importing thousands of seasonal outsiders who would stay confined to their chalets, we wanted to create a small, walkable village for people from around the globe to enjoy, and blend that with our existing community. Everyone would be able to gather and grow for decades to come. That seemed to be the perfect hybrid: develop *and* maintain.

Not surprisingly, this unique outlook boxed us into a difficult situation. Hardly any institutional financing was going to be available to us because we weren't maxing out on density. No bank would write us a loan. Nobody would invest equity. It meant we had to find an alternative path to pull together the money to buy Powder Mountain and build our new dream.

We had to remind ourselves to be realistic. We still didn't know how much the mountain would cost, or if we could possibly afford it.

We called our old partner, Ryan, for advice.

He had worked in private equity before joining Elliott's dad's business. He really understood real estate, having bought and sold many major properties in his time at a prestigious fund.

"Very risky," he said. "Very, *very* risky."

Brett also sensed we were running out of time to take that risk. The world was still in the tail end of the Great Recession, which had put everything on pause. The lending for speculative real estate projects outside of major cities was still frozen.

We soon learned that twenty other prospective buyers had toured Powder Mountain in the hope of buying it, but eventually passed. They were worried it'd be a huge amount of work to turn it into a mass-market project. There wasn't enough preexisting infrastructure, or enough amenities in town. The buyer would've had to build a dozen restaurants and retail outlets in order to support ten thousand units of real estate. It was a lot of development and investment, on top of the asking price for the mountain itself.

But the village we mapped out on the whiteboard wasn't some Disney on Ice theme park. It would be small, intimate, and self-sustaining. We wanted the raw, rugged nature to remain intact. The idea was to build in sync with the surroundings, to make a small environmental footprint that would preserve the natural habitats. This approach couldn't have been more different from putting up ten thousand units and building the infrastructure needed to support all the people that would occupy them. It meant much less infrastructure, much less retail, and fewer restaurants—which meant less money for us to put down up front.

It had been more than three years since the height of the 2008 recession. Perhaps it would have been ideal for us to wait a few more years before trying to take such a huge leap, but we sensed the landscape would change soon. With the economy springing back, someone might casually drop in and happily buy the mountain for double or triple the price—whatever the price was. *Now* was our time.

We called Ryan again in New York from our house in Malibu, trying to get him excited about the opportunity. *"Very, very risky,"* Ryan reminded us. *"Very, very, very risky."*

It had been nearly a month since our visit to Powder Mountain, and by this point, we had already sketched out a shell of an idea for what we wanted to build. But we still had no clue how much the whole thing would cost.

Finally, one evening, during one of our late-night whiteboard sessions, Elliott's phone lit up with a call from Greg.

When it did, we ran toward him and huddled around the chair he was sitting in.

"So, is it just a rumor or is it actually for sale?" we asked. "What's the deal?"

"All right," Greg said, "we can buy the mountain . . . for $40 million."

32

IT'S NOT ABOUT THE IDEA.
IT'S ABOUT THE EXECUTION.

The four of us spent the next several days bouncing between unbridled enthusiasm and overwhelming anxiety. We were beside ourselves about potentially finding the
permanent home for Summit. But there were a few slight
complications. One, we didn't have $40 million. Two, most
people thought we were insane.

We didn't blame them. Our company had about $1 mil-
lion in the bank, and it was earmarked to pay everybody's
salaries. How were we going to buy a mountain for $40 mil-
lion without an institutional loan?

The private equity firm that was selling the mountain
couldn't make good on their investment. Their development
plans had been stalled in the Utah Supreme Court, and the
surrounding community was up in arms. Plus, because it
was the tail end of the recession, no one—let alone ten thousand people—wanted to buy a second home. The firm was
struggling, and it wanted out. Very sophisticated people

were throwing in the towel. Who were we to think we could pull it off if they couldn't?

We needed help, so we started to put our feelers out for advice. We've never been the type to keep secrets. If you keep your cards too close to your chest, you're not going to get mentorship from the world, and it's going to take you a lot longer to accomplish what you set out to do.

One of the other reasons people often keep quiet about big plans is that they're worried someone else will try to beat them to it. But who, upon hearing that we wanted to buy a random mountain with no infrastructure in place, was suddenly going to pounce on a block of land they'd never seen in rural Utah?

Our idea seemed so audacious we weren't worried about anyone stealing it. We've long believed that entrepreneurs lose a great deal by not sharing their ideas out of fear of having them ripped off. Nobody is really thinking about the same thing you're thinking about, let alone plotting to steal your idea to monetize it. Even if they tried, could they be more successful at it than you?

The idea *alone* is not what's valuable. The real value comes later, through hard work and execution. There's a great, albeit violent, observation from the physicist Howard Aiken that backs this up: "Don't worry about people stealing your ideas. If your ideas are any good, you'll have to ram them down people's throats." It's way more likely that people will line up to tell you everything that's wrong with your idea than it is that they'll try to scoop it out from under you.

The land on Powder Mountain was nearly three-fourths the size of Manhattan: ten thousand acres. Most of that land—eight thousand acres—made up the ski resort. By pur-

chasing the mountain, we'd take over ownership and management of the ski resort. On the backside of the mountain,
outside the boundaries of the resort, we planned to build our
village on just forty of the acres.

As we worked to get a letter of intent—an agreement that
stated our intention to purchase the mountain—we needed
to come up with a unique way of building excitement, awareness, and ultimately financing to purchase the property. But
we couldn't even legally sell these hypothetical homesites:
In order to sell real estate, you need to own the property, and
we didn't yet. That property then has to be entitled and
zoned, which takes time, and on top of that you need roads,
water, sewers, and power. We were a long way from owning
the property, and it would take another couple of years before we could install these basic utilities. So we needed to
sell people on the *idea* of $40 million worth of ski homes
without any knowledge of when they would actually be able
to build their houses.

We spent the following months trying to figure out a
strategy. By now it was December, and we felt like we were
running up against a wall. Basecamp was less than two
months away, and we hadn't figured out how to raise a single
penny to buy the property.

Then, we stumbled across a concept that would change
everything.

We found out about something called a "founding member program." It's been implemented countless times in the
founding of golf communities. At first glance, it's complicated, because you're asking people to put up millions of dollars. But when it's laid out alongside drawings of homesites
and a master plan of the community, people can see the vision and find it really compelling.

So we got to work with our lawyers and put together an initial concept. Here's how the program worked: Instead of buying a home the traditional way, the founding members who put up the money would sign a hundred-page document that entitled them to a homesite *credit,* as well as benefits once the homesites were ready to be sold.

When the founding members put down a deposit for a homesite credit, their money would land in an escrow account with our law firm for their protection. We needed to hit a series of milestones to be allowed to draw down any of their money from that escrow account. For example, only *after* there was $20 million in the escrow account, and *after* we got a letter of intent from the county for a bond, and *after* our entitlements were completed would our law firm be able to release that $20 million as a down payment to buy the mountain. The seller agreed that the remaining $20 million would be paid over time.

With our founding member program in place, we now had a renewed source of momentum. Our founding members would have security and comfort in their investments; we couldn't just take their money and then not buy the mountain. If we didn't raise the $20 million, they'd get their money back.

We believed it was now actually possible to pull the whole thing off: We didn't need $40 million all at once. Yes, we still had to come up with $20 million, but it would buy us time to figure out how to raise the remaining $20 million over several years.

The fact that we thought $20 million sounded like a reasonable number should demonstrate just how unreasonable we were. But we felt like we were moving in the right direction. With our plan in place, we decided it was time to share the vision with our whole team.

We set up a dinner at the Malibu house and instructed everyone to wear their best 1970s-themed ski outfits. Everybody came in vibrant mountain sweaters, ski hats, and vintage onesies. We served our team a meal that included fondue and hot chocolate, and after dinner, we got a drumbeat rolling on the table.

"Okay, everyone," Jeremy began. "First and foremost, thank you for choosing to commit yourselves to this shared vision of Summit. As far as we know, we only get one life to live, and we honor and respect the fact that you've chosen to take a chance with us."

"We've discovered the next step in our journey," Jeff jumped in.

"We're buying a mountain!" Elliott blurted out.

The drumroll abruptly came to a halt.

Elliott's statement didn't have the desired effect. We were hoping that the team would leap up in cheers. Instead, there were scrunched foreheads and confused looks around the table.

"What do you mean?" someone asked.

"You know, a mountain. We're buying a mountain," Brett said. "After Summit Basecamp, we're going to move the company and team to a small town in Utah called Eden. The biggest ski resort that no one has ever heard of in the United States, called Powder Mountain, is for sale."

"We're going to build a permanent home there for the Summit community!" Elliott chimed in.

After a few more moments of lingering silence, the concept began to slowly sink in with everyone.

"You're all serious? We're going to buy a mountain?"

As reality set in, the energy began to shift. People started clapping, banging on the tables, and cheering.

If the four of us had any reservations about our ability to pull off such an outlandish idea, they were quickly washed away by our team. We believed in them and they believed in us. That level of trust and understanding creates the foundation needed to accomplish any large feat.

We spent the next two months sharing the idea with close friends and trusted mentors and tweaking the founding member program to ensure we could raise the money we needed. Then we got ready to unveil our plans at Basecamp.

We put together a PowerPoint presentation to share on the final day of the event. But as we rehearsed, we felt it was falling flat. It was impossible to translate our vision and what we had seen on top of that mountain into a few slides of a deck. We realized we needed people to experience the mountain for themselves. What could be more compelling than standing on top of the world looking out over an expansive mountain range?

So, seven days before Basecamp was to kick off, we scrapped the presentation entirely and dreamed up a new plan to try to blow people's minds. What if we could organize a *second* event to be held at Powder Mountain? What if we could transport a core group of community members riding high on the tail end of Basecamp directly to the top of Powder Mountain to reveal our future plans for Summit?

We got to work. Instead of presenting our idea to all eight hundred attendees at the event, we decided to focus on just sixty of our biggest supporters. If our concept could shock and awe them, we felt it would snowball from there.

With only a week to spare, we began to assemble a mini-Summit in Eden—on top of all the final preparations for Basecamp. For starters, we needed a location on the top of the mountain for a barrel fire, and a place where people could warm up if it got cold or windy. At the moment, there was *nothing* up there. No toilets. No shelter. So we called the general manager of the mountain and asked if he'd be open to building us a hut. We had met him briefly during our initial tour and, luckily, he had taken a liking to us. He agreed.

Zoning regulations limited the size of an unapproved structure to under 150 square feet, and it couldn't be fixed in the ground. So the Powder Mountain staff showed they could innovate just as well as the entrepreneurs in the Summit community: They built one on skis so it could move around.

Not everything went so smoothly. While we were piecing together the details of our mini-Summit, we ran into a logistical headache. We wanted the guests' transition from Tahoe to Eden to be as quick and seamless as possible. The airport near Lake Tahoe was only an eighty-minute flight to Ogden, Utah, which was then a twenty-five-minute drive to Powder Mountain. There was just one problem: Commercial flights didn't fly that route. We'd need to charter our own plane.

Piece of cake, we figured. We'd chartered a cruise ship before. Maybe we could get a couple of prop planes to shuttle back and forth. After some research, we quickly discovered a prop plane wasn't going to cut it for sixty passengers. We needed something *much* bigger. Like a 737. That posed all sorts of other problems. But, without time to come up with another solution, we knew it was the only viable option. This trip from Tahoe to Powder Mountain was our one shot to show the community our plans for the future and hopefully get their support in the process.

So, without having the plane locked in or even a good sense of how much it'd cost, we pressed onward. We personally wrote letters to the sixty people we identified as our biggest supporters. We asked each of them to join us for an all-expenses-paid weekend to a surprise destination. Yes, we said *all expenses paid.* It was déjà vu: We were doing what Elliott had done when he offered to fly that original group of people first-class to his first event in Utah. This time we promised bonfires, s'mores, and hot tubs—and more than one case of beer.

We told them that when Basecamp ended, a bus would depart from the back of the hotel for the Reno-Tahoe International Airport at 10 A.M. sharp (we hadn't even confirmed with the flight charter company if this time would work). Little did they know that the four of us and our advance team, along with sixty fellow guests, would arrive at a gate with only the plane's tail number on the *departures* display screen and board a chartered 737 headed to an undisclosed location. The gate at the airport would be a little like Platform 9¾ from the Harry Potter books: Nobody else could see it, only the people boarding the train on that platform.

We packed up the house in Malibu, once again condensing our belongings down to one suitcase each, and donated the additional items we'd accrued over the last nine months to the Salvation Army.

As we loaded up the cars to head to the airport for Tahoe, we got an overwhelming feeling that this might be the last time our team would ever move. The feeling lasted for only a second before our attention snapped back to the nearly insurmountable task ahead of us. We were heading into our annual version of the Super Bowl, while having to prepare for a World Series just a few days later.

But the train was now in motion and there was no getting off.

33

UNITE THE CORE TO MOVE THE MASSES

There was something different about Basecamp compared to any of the events preceding it—something we felt as soon as we arrived at the hotel in Lake Tahoe on a snowy afternoon.

We got to work building out the event. This time, our team was putting together massive stages made of flat reclaimed wood that fit on poles and easily snapped together. No more frantically calling New Jersey after midnight and asking for missing nuts and bolts. This time, there *were* no nuts and bolts—and no bloodied hands either. We were prepared and working smoothly as one cohesive unit. You could say we finally had all our flags ironed.

Unlike previous events, where we'd built out a few hotel ballrooms, in Tahoe we took over the entire resort. Within forty-eight hours, the event was completely assembled. We walked around and marveled at the geodesic dome constructed for a session called "Curving Your Perspective." We stopped at the barbershop we'd created for attendees to step in for a haircut and coffee. We all smiled as we walked through a hidden door in a broom closet to access a custom-built 1920s speakeasy, complete with a period jukebox, soundtrack, and craft cocktail bar.

When we looked at the beautiful structures our team had created, it felt so unfortunate that they would live for only three and a half days. We held on to the hope that soon all of these amazing architectural feats would have a permanent home.

By this stage, most of the attendees knew us well. Many knew how we'd cut our hands putting together the stage for DC10. Many had danced during the blackout when The Roots sapped too much power from the engine room at Summit at Sea. But as soon as they arrived at Basecamp, they could see the leap we'd made in engineering and architecture. Then they dove into a weekend filled with immersive experiences. There were yoga classes from one of our favorite instructors, Elena Brower; talks from varied folks, ranging from Diplo to the president of the country Georgia; and intimate performances from Aloe Blacc, José González, and Metric.

One night we shuttled guests, bundled in their jackets and hats, to the top of the mountain in a tram. As they approached the top, they could hear the faint sounds of Questlove spinning at the peak. The music got louder and louder as they reached the summit and walked into a lodge we'd taken over for the evening. We called it "Beats at 9,000 Feet."

Basecamp would have seemed like a major success on its own. But while the event was playing out, we were frantically booking an entirely different event on an entirely different mountain to be held in three days. While attendees celebrated and danced the night away, we had team members in a windowless conference room trying to line up the plane we'd already promised would be waiting at our meta- phorical Platform 9¾.

"How much will it cost to charter a 737?"

David Blaine, who'd once been encased in a block of ice for more than sixty-three consecutive hours in Times Square, strolled the hallways of Basecamp and did one-on-one magic tricks for everyone he encountered. Or so we heard—we were too busy scrambling to find a venue in Eden.

"Can we rent a house for sixty? . . . When? Oh, in two days."

Rescued mountain lions surprised attendees at a nature talk called "Narnia Meets Walden."

"No, no, no. That's thirty rental cars we'll need!"

Rohan Oza, the "Hollywood Brandfather" behind Vita- minwater, gave a marketing masterclass.

"We'll need those cars waiting on the tarmac at the airport in Ogden."

Basecamp attendees rolled their own sushi with a Michelin-star-awarded Japanese chef.

"And we'll need plates for sixty. And silverware!"

Musicians jammed on the piano in the speakeasy late into the night, rocking singalong after singalong.

"Oh, and can we put this all on a credit card, by chance?"

The crowd celebrated at the closing party to hip-hop roy- alty DJ Jazzy Jeff and Q-Tip.

"So, the 737 is confirmed for Monday morning at eleven!"

We had never chartered a private jet before, and we had just rented a 737 from a commercial airline.

After three days jammed with performances, talks, and celebration, Basecamp came to a successful conclusion. The morning after the event, the sixty core community members who'd received the handwritten invitations jumped on their designated bus and met us at the Reno airport.

Loud chatter filled the terminal as our attendees worked their way through the concourse, riding high from the weekend and wondering about what they were about to experience. The four of us stood at the gate, smiling, as the raucous crowd poured past us and onto the plane. Once aboard, we welcomed everyone to Summit Air, told them the flight time would be eighty minutes, and hoped that they'd sit back, relax, and enjoy the flight.

The passengers were diving into animated conversations with each other and shouting at new friends five rows up. Unfortunately, we couldn't be as relaxed. We had planned to show everyone the jaw-dropping view as the sun set over Powder Mountain, but we were running behind schedule. We started to worry that when we got to the mountain the only thing our guests would find was total darkness.

As soon as we landed on the tarmac, the four of us knew that we were within fifteen minutes of botching the entire unveiling. We wrangled everyone into the rental cars as fast as possible and took off for the mountain. Luckily, the guests were so engaged with one another that they didn't sense our apprehension.

The caravan of rental cars arrived at the top of the mountain just as the sun sent pink, orange, and red streaks across the sky. As soon as everyone stepped out, the chatter that had been going on for hours immediately stopped. Everyone stood in awe and stared out toward the mountain peaks in the distance.

"You might be wondering what you're doing up here. As many of you know, we've wanted to find a permanent home for Summit for a long time. Six months ago, we came to this spot and stood right where you're standing," Jeff said, sweeping his hand out behind him, "looking out at this . . ."

His pause invited everyone to gaze out over the Great Salt Lake and the divide in the Wasatch Mountains, where the view extended over four states. Silence hung in the air.

"We knew in that moment that Summit's home should be a literal summit. *This* summit. It's where we're going to create a physical place for Summit that represents our community's values. Supporting this community is our life's purpose. We're going to build a place where people from around the world can form friendships, where their families can spend time together, and where their kids can grow up and start families of their own. And we want you to be part of that story with us."

As the sun set and darkness came over the mountain, a roaring fire near the 144-square-foot hut accented the moment. Everybody understood that they'd been brought in at the very start, and that we saw them as our closest supporters who shared our values. A deep feeling of being part of something special was all around us.

Later that evening, everyone drove down the mountain to the valley below and gathered at the lake house we had frantically secured just days prior. We hosted a family-style dinner and everyone talked late into the night, sharing ideas and dreams of what this place could be.

We didn't just tell our core supporters about our plans for Powder Mountain—we showed them. We'd carefully crafted a narrative that would create a story, starting with those personalized letters. That had got them to the plane without knowing where they were going, and a caravan of cars had led them to the same spot on top of Powder Mountain where the four of us had first seen the view, exactly as the sun was setting. The ritual had included us making a fire on top of the mountain and breaking bread together. These decisions were all designed to enhance the texture of memory, to create the maximum sense of romance possible. Guests could see how much we valued them, as well as the level of care we were bringing to this project.

By the end of the weekend, everyone was asking how they could help build this community with us. We told everyone no photos were allowed. They could tell as many people as they wanted in person, but they couldn't email anyone about it or post on social media. We wanted it to be shared one-on-one.

We'd learned just how crucial this strategy was when it came to creating momentum. It's so important to bring your biggest supporters in from the start. *Unite the core to move the masses.* Those first guests would become our best storytellers and most valuable messengers, allowing our idea to gain traction and spread out to a wider group of people. With the daunting task ahead of us, we were going to need all the momentum we could get.

34

BECOME A FAVOR ECONOMY
MILLIONAIRE

In high school, one of the best feelings we all remember is that moment when you hand in your last final exam. You've been studying and stressing for weeks leading up to that day, laser-focused on what needed to be accomplished and the facts that needed to be memorized. And then, when that last paper is handed in, it's all over, just like that. You can relax, breathe easy, and enjoy your summer vacation.

For a moment, that's exactly how we felt. Except it was the dead of winter, late January 2012, and there was a foot of snow blanketing the lawn we looked out upon from the lake house window.

Normally, after a big event, we'd take the month off to relax, travel, and catch up on sleep. But that wasn't an option this time. The letter of intent we'd signed to purchase Powder Mountain stated that the $20 million deposit was due in less than six months. That gave us hardly any time to come up with the cash. Considering that the most money we'd ever raised up until this point was $1 million for a marine protected area in the Bahamas, we knew we had our work cut out for us. There wasn't a moment to waste.

We looked at each other, then around the cavernous fifteen-thousand-square-foot cabin made of supersized logs, and smiled, settling into the idea that this would be our new home for the foreseeable future. Our days of beach house living were over. We strolled through the sprawling second floor, surveying each bedroom to determine pricing, and then split up the rooms among our team yet again. Within a week, the cabin became our home, our office, and our hosting space.

During our first week in the cabin, we followed up with the sixty guests we had just hosted. Every single one was still reeling from the weekend, inspired by what they had experienced. They told us that they were trying to explain the mountain to their friends but felt their words weren't doing it justice.

"You really just need to go there," they'd say, "and experience it for yourself."

This gave us an idea. We definitely didn't know the fine details of buying a mountain and resort, but one thing we *did* know was how to gather people and create unforgettable experiences. We knew that in order to buy the mountain, we'd need to create widespread awareness and buy-in from our community. What better way to do so than host them in our new mountain town to showcase our vision?

Our entire team began reaching out to everyone in the Summit community, inviting them to come spend time at the mountain. We took the concept of the first weekend with sixty guests and soon expanded it to two hundred people every weekend.

We'd bring our guests to the top of the mountain as the

burnt-orange sunset crawled across the sky. We'd huddle everyone together and talk about our hopes and dreams for what we wanted to build. We'd then come back to the lake house and personally serve farm-to-table dinners made up of ingredients procured within five miles of our new home. It felt like our dinners in Malibu on overdrive. More importantly, it felt authentic and real, because it was. We wanted to build intimacy, because intimacy and vulnerability build trust. We knew if we could build trust under this roof, people were likely going to want to be part of what we were creating.

While we could choreograph a good story, the truth is, aside from gathering guests every weekend, we had absolutely no clue about how to move ahead on Powder Mountain. Acquiring a massive stretch of land was an entirely different beast. We didn't even know what we didn't know.

It was around this time that we discovered we were favor-economy millionaires.

What does that mean? Well, we believe there are two economies. There's the cash economy that we all know well, the one built on capitalism, clever marketing campaigns, and retail therapy. And then there's the favor economy. The favor economy is made up of the relationships you have that allow you to access expertise and opportunities, built upon a foundation of what you've been able to do for others. We didn't have much actual money—but we did have plenty of friends and favors to call in. And those are priceless.

Over the years, we'd made many helpful connections for many people in many different disciplines. People we'd connected had started companies together, had raised money for nonprofits, and had even met their future spouse. We saw life as a giving competition, not a game of trades or a reciprocity loop. And if you're genuinely giving without the expectation of return, you create the ability to ask the same of other people. We called it the Triangulation of Goodwill.

It's very different from only doing favors when there's something in it for you. Rest assured, if you're a quid pro quo networker, the world is going to come right back at you the same way. But if you're giving out of the goodness of your heart, because it makes you feel good, you can create the Triangulation of Goodwill. This gave us permission to ask for all the help we needed. The recipients of all the goodwill that we'd extended over the years and all the connections we'd made for them were now thrilled to come through for us.

"Let me introduce you to a world-class architect," one would say.

"I can get you to an amazing mountain developer," offered another.

We needed to learn about development, zoning, land conservation, entitlements, county bonds, sewage, roads, and much more. We were stepping into a twilight zone of 160-point due-diligence checklists on topics we had no understanding of.

We had chartered a cruise liner. We had rented a commercial jet. But we had never tried to buy a mountain.

We needed the best people to help us because the stakes for getting things wrong were now *much* higher. If we made a mistake at an event—which we did all the time—we could quickly recover. The show must go on, right? That's a completely different dynamic from building physical infrastructure for a growing community that will endure for generations. We were not going to have the luxury of installing a ski lift in the wrong spot or the ability to change our minds about where to place a road. Either of those things would cost us millions of dollars, hundreds of unhappy neighbors, and perhaps the whole project.

We got our first taste of how complicated things were going to be when we were introduced to a venture capitalist who we thought could help us out. He'd done a development project for entrepreneurs in Silicon Valley, so we thought that if anyone would understand what we aspired to do, he'd be the guy—and maybe he'd even want to come in as a partner.

It didn't start well.

"I don't like it," he said bluntly. "First, you're going to run into development costs. It's death by a thousand cuts. There are thousands of line items. Contractors aren't incentivized to spend less, they're incentivized to spend more so they can charge you more. You're gonna get crushed on change orders. And if it's not the change orders, you'll get blocked by some obscure local ordinance. Someone's gonna point out that this particular area has a right-of-way grandfathered in for some particular family you've never met who has lived nearby for two hundred years, and you won't be able to develop there. Or PETA will tell you that this is the habitat for some rare beaver and they will get an environmental stop order on your development."

By the end of the meeting, he was practically standing up and yelling at us: *"The ordinances are going to destroy you!"*

We were twenty-six and twenty-seven years old. We'd got to where we were through sheer willpower, boldness, and hustle, but that wasn't going to cut it anymore. We quickly understood that this would not be as simple as getting people to invest money into our idea, hiring a team to design our village, and then hiring a contractor to build it.

Just when we began to realize how clueless we were,

Beth Comstock, then the SVP at General Electric, jumped in to lift us up without distorting our reality.

"Guys, you know I adore you. However, I think it's clear that you aren't currently capable of handling this alone," she said. "But I believe in your capacity to lean into the curve, take the knocks that are inevitable in a project of this scale, and actually make this happen."

Beth's confidence in us told us it was *okay* to not know everything we needed to know. What was important was that we be brutally honest with ourselves in identifying the specific areas in which we were clueless, such as tax-increment financing, water rights, and municipal bonds, and *immediately* begin learning about them.

At the same time, we needed to continue showcasing our idea to as many people from our community as possible, and convince a small percentage to invest in homes through our founding member program. The last was obviously the most difficult. While people in our community wanted to get behind us, many weren't in the market for a house on a mountaintop in Utah. Just because you love or support an idea doesn't mean it's right for you.

Each weekend, we'd practice and refine our pitch to any of our guests who'd shown interest in the project, and who we thought might want to invest. To our amazement, every single person said no. Elliott had flashbacks to the first event in Park City and found the conversations he was having to be eerily similar.

"I'm very interested! But let me see who else invests. Circle back with me early next year."

"I love the vision! I can't wait to buy a home once you already own the mountain."

No one wanted to be the first one in the pool.

Then one day, a couple of months into the winter season, a big champion of ours from Guatemala showed up to one of our weekends.

Matias de Tezanos had been twenty years old when he founded the most-visited Spanish-language hotel reservation site, Hoteles.com, back in 2000. He sold it two years later to Expedia. He'd later set up and sold a digital advertising network in Latin America that was acquired by News Corp, and then founded an investment group called People-Fund that primarily invested in tech start-ups. In March 2012, when he showed up at Powder Mountain, he had recently been named one of the top ten Hispanic entrepreneurs by *Inc.* magazine.

We gave Matias the "coolest mountain town in the world" pitch, describing how we were going to preserve the pristine natural beauty, acquire the ski resort, and build a thoughtfully designed town that would support entrepreneurs and artists.

At this point, we still didn't have a single commitment to the project. Not even one of the sixty people we had first brought to the mountaintop had come through and committed. We trudged through our pitch to Matias, expecting him to grill us with a hundred questions we didn't have answers to and then to give us the response we'd been getting from everyone else: *Sounds exciting, but it's not quite the right fit.*

Then out of nowhere, Matias boomed, "I love it! Sounds amazing! I'm in for two million. I'm going to wire you a million dollars this week and a million dollars next week."

We were stunned. "Okay. Um, amazing. Thank you! There is just one small issue: We don't technically have all the deal terms fully worked out or the timeframe in which we can pa—"

"We'll figure that out later," he said with a smile. "As an entrepreneur, nobody actually believes in you at the very beginning when you need it the most. So I'm going to be that person, because I *do* believe in you. I'm going to be your first investor."

We felt like someone had just lifted a fifty-pound weight off our chests that we hadn't even known was there. We could breathe again. We felt rejuvenated, like we might actually be able to pull this thing off.

In the back of our minds we wondered why we'd received so many nos from so many people with the exact same pitch that excited Matias. As if seeing the bewilderment on our faces, he chimed in and told us he wasn't just investing in a house on Powder Mountain—he was investing in all of us. As a longtime Summit attendee, he explained that he'd never found a place where he could be himself until he found Summit. So the idea that Summit could have a permanent home was really attractive to him. He then shared a short story with us. "I'll tell you what my first investor told me," he said. "If you lose all my money, you'll make me double on the next one!" He knew we were going to be successful eventually. It might not be on this project, and it might not be the next one. But he recognized that the hardest time was now.

Matias became our first founding member. And we stood in amazement as he told us he didn't want any of his money to go into the escrow account—he wanted us to spend his money immediately so we could turn our dreams into a reality. We could use that capital to host events that brought in more prospective founding members, as well as hire additional consultants to give us crash courses in real estate development.

Matias gave us our liftoff. We organized a weekly series

of charrettes (intense periods of design or planning) to help us speed up the process. We brought in developers, architects, land planners, master planners, membership experts, and a whole team of consultants to help us come up with ideas.

Every Thursday night, our charrettes would wrap up, and we'd begin hosting the two hundred guests who arrived for the weekend event. After a long weekend of high-energy activities, the guests would depart Sunday night. Then the next round of charrettes would start again on Monday morning. This went on week after week through winter, spring, and into summer.

No matter how exhausted we were, we'd make sure to greet our guests with an excited smile. We truly were grateful that they'd chosen to spend their time with us that weekend.

We kept giving and giving and giving with the full belief that whatever we needed would come back to us. And eventually it did—just not in the way we expected.

35

FIND THE TIPPING DOMINO

Raising the money to purchase Powder Mountain was the most complicated task we'd ever faced. Though we were close to perfecting the Summit playbook for events, we couldn't use it for this game. There was, however, one small similarity.

Back in the early days of Summit, when people had no idea who we were, they didn't necessarily trust what we were doing. It took a lot of work to convince people to attend our early Aspen and Miami events. We had discovered that although they might not trust *us*, they most certainly trusted their *friends*. We knew if we could get one person to say yes, then their friends were more likely to say yes as well. It wasn't the event that really mattered; it was the people with whom you were experiencing it.

We decided to see if we could apply that same logic to the mountain. We realized that pitching all the advantages of ski-in/ski-out homes and farm-to-table dining experiences wasn't enough. People ultimately wanted to know who their neighbors were going to be.

This forced us to change the way we were approaching our Powder Mountain homesite offering. Before selling registrations to our events, we'd ask ourselves, *Who is the best speaker or performer we can get?* Now we were asking, *Who is the most compelling neighbor one could possibly have? Who would we want to live next to, have over for morning coffee, or share après-ski drinks with?*

We brainstormed a list of entrepreneurs, musicians, pro athletes, authors, and other creatives we'd want to spend time with, and began inviting them to the mountain.

One of the people on our list was Richard Branson. Who could possibly be more fun to have as a neighbor than Richard?

But it wasn't that simple. When you're reaching out to someone who already has everything, a sweet deal just isn't that compelling. You can send Michael Jordan a box of sneakers from your new shoe company or a free time-share in your golf community, but it's doubtful he's going to wear your kicks or play eighteen holes.

Many things would have to go right for Richard to say yes. Not only would he have to *like* Powder Mountain, but he'd have to want a mountain home in Utah, believe in our vision, and feel comfortable putting his name behind it.

When we pitched him on it, he seemed surprisingly receptive. But he said he'd have to bring it up with his entire team. It was a while before he talked to them about it, and when he finally did, everyone was opposed.

Elliott received a phone call from one of Richard's team members.

"Look," she told Elliott, "we respect you guys. But our job

is to protect Richard. He's already successful. Our job is to *not* lose his money. Our job is to *not* mess up his brand." Looking for a soft landing, she added, "We love what you're doing, and Richard actually told us that you remind him of himself when he was your age."

Elliott couldn't resist basking in the compliment. *Wow. I'm a young Richard Branson!* he thought. *I'm a visionary!*

But his daydream was harshly ended by the exec's interpretation: "Yeah, you do remind us of Richard when he was your age—young and naive."

Richard was a no.

We realized we were trying to sell people on a dream that existed only in our minds. We couldn't even begin to build homes, pave a single road, or plant a tree until we put down the money to close the deal. And even if we did come up with the money, it would take at least a year to design and plan the new homes, and then an additional eighteen months to build them. That construction could happen only once we had plotted and titled all of the real estate, secured water rights, approved zoning, and hooked each homesite up to power, water, and sewage. For a long time, we'd be selling a concept on a whiteboard.

Convincing members of our community to join our dream was not going to happen overnight. How long would it take to get the financial support we needed? Three months? Six months? A year, or even *two*? We didn't have that kind of time.

We continued to host our two-hundred-person gatherings every weekend at the mountain. This created a cadence, a pattern that demonstrated to everyone that when they showed up they'd see old friends and meet new ones. Everyone would return to their homes in distant cities and organize their own events to keep the conversations and collaborations going. Although we were hemorrhaging money by making the events free, the community felt stronger than ever.

But we needed something more. We needed to give a glimpse into what our mountain town might *feel* like ten years down the road. We needed people to experience our vision in real time, while also showcasing our momentum in reaching our goal. If we could somehow pull that off, we believed, it would convince people to invest in us.

So we used $500,000 of Matias's investment to renovate the entire basement of the lake house. We didn't own the home, but we knew the investment was crucial in showcasing the types of experiences we planned to create on the mountain. We built a spa with massage rooms and a massive steam room, along with steps leading up to two newly installed hot tubs overlooking the lake. We created an ashram with plush pillows and billowing ceiling fabric for yoga, meditation, and tea ceremonies. We converted four thousand square feet into a floor-to-ceiling oak speakeasy with well-appointed furniture, a long wooden bar, and a stage with a state-of-the-art sound system for live performances. It was a small taste of our vision, but it was now available for guests to immerse themselves in when they showed up on weekends. Now our dream started to feel real to them.

Momentum is a powerful tool. It creates feelings of excitement, it compounds trust, and it instills a sense of urgency. When people can feel the energy of something building upon itself, they want to be a part of it.

We figured that even an accumulation of small but incremental developments would allow everyone in our network to see real and consistent progress.

So we began to let our community know about new hires, new neighbors, and upcoming events through weekly newsletters and phone calls. When we touted our next free weekend, we'd tell people about the updated family-style kitchen table we'd installed, the new steam room, and our newly completed ashram. We'd tell people about our research trip to see four Alpine mountain towns in Switzerland, and the takeaways that we'd apply to Powder Mountain. We mentioned how the legendary architect Tom Kundig had flown in and was sketching designs for a future lodge. We quoted the lead designer of Hart Howerton, one of the most well-regarded land-planning firms in America, saying that this was "one of the most exciting projects they'd ever worked on."

The strategy started to work. Slowly, more people began to invest in our founding member program.

As money trickled in, we worked out extensions on the final closing date of the purchase contract and continued to negotiate the purchase price down. This was essentially a much more complex version of what happens during the due diligence of purchasing a new home. *Two toilets are broken and need to be replaced, and it looks like we need a new sewer line. We're going to have to take money off the purchase price.* Anyone who's bought or sold a home knows how the inspection and wrangling process goes, but it's infinitely more complicated with a property of this size.

Our stress levels were ten times higher than at any event we'd ever thrown, and we went out of contract *seven times* during the negotiations. The seller had agreed to extend the original contract's six-month term in order to allow us to come up with the money. But each time we extended it, we would have to put large sums of hard money down in order to keep the deal alive. We'd blow past the due date, feeling completely defeated, like it was all over, only to miraculously find another founding member who believed in us.

We were making headway, but we still needed to delay the closing date because we hadn't yet raised all the money to make the down payment. It was late fall, the air was getting crisp, and the leaves had long lost their vibrant colors and were starting to fall. Things were looking bleak.

Then one day, Elliott received an email that changed everything: "We're pleased to confirm Richard Branson's involvement in the project." Apparently the momentum we'd displayed had become more and more attractive to Richard's team over the last several months.

Elliott jumped up from his desk and sprinted to the kitchen to find the three of us making sandwiches.

"You guys—Richard's in!"

"Richard who?" Jeremy asked.

"Richard *Branson*."

Brett slammed his sandwich down on the table in excitement, drawing team members out of their rooms in curiosity.

"Feels good to know that Richard Branson is our new neighbor," Jeff said, letting out a sigh of relief.

Having Richard join our community communicated a lot to the world. If Richard Branson and his team were participating in the project, others might now also consider being founding members.

That moment was a huge win for us. But the race was far from over.

36

PRESSURE MAKES DIAMONDS

We sensed we needed one final burst of momentum to get the deal done, and so we were relieved to see the snow falling again as winter approached toward the end of 2012.

Although we'd gone out of contract numerous times, the owners were growing more and more confident that we'd be able to close on the deal. We explained to them that the more control we had over the experience for our potential investors, the better the likelihood of getting everything wrapped up quickly. This seemed to satisfy them. In a sign of goodwill, they offered us the managerial keys to the ski resort, even though we still hadn't technically signed on the dotted line.

That meant we could present the crown jewel of ski experiences to everyone who visited, offering free lift tickets and private snowcat rides. John Legend visited the mountain that winter and took over our lake house on Thanksgiving with his family. One of the founders of Google, Sergey Brin,

joined us for a weekend. Ann Veneman, who had left UNI-
CEF and joined the board of Nestlé, came in as a founding
member. So did Gayle Troberman, soon to be CMO of iHeart-
Radio and former chief creative officer of Microsoft. And our
old friends Tim Ferriss and Blake Mycoskie got behind us to
invest as well. Ashton Kutcher brought out Kevin Systrom,
the founder of Instagram, along with a bunch of other great
founders for a backcountry ski trip. It was safe to say the
project's momentum was starting to pick up as we headed
deeper into winter.

Everything felt like it was coming together. We had ver-
bal agreements from more than ten people, but we needed at
least another dozen founding members to make the down
payment.

It was time to reach out to the press and tell the entire
world what we were doing, to set up our final sprint to the
finish line.

We arranged the announcement of the sale the way every
other reputable company breaks the news to the media. The
idea is to control the narrative and avoid leaks. Typically, you
say that the company has reached "a definitive agreement to
make a purchase." This kind of legal jargon is common in
newspapers and business newsletters.

There was one slight difference between our press release and that of thousands of other companies in our position. For example, when Google announces it has reached a
definitive agreement to make a purchase of a tech company,
everyone knows it's simply a matter of finishing the due diligence process before it takes control of the start-up. In our
case, we still had to come up with a lot of the money to close
the deal.

We were still millions of dollars short. Even the money

that had come in on the homesite credits we *had* sold was on shaky ground. While some founders like Matias had paid upfront straight into our bank accounts, other founders had taken a cautious approach and put up refundable 25 percent deposits, which went into the escrow account. In theory, that meant we'd get the full 100 percent over time. But for now, only a quarter of the total sale was placed in the escrow account. Simply put, we could have brought in $40 million worth of founding members, but only have $10 million available to us in the account. What's more, the whole amount could be removed at a moment's notice with an email to our law firm from a founding member if people changed their minds. As a result, the numbers were not absolute.

We were banking on the press announcement to push the entire process toward its conclusion. The way we saw it, there was no going back. The embarrassment of announcing too soon and failing to close paled in comparison to the reputational liability we had already taken on within the Summit community. There was no option but to forge ahead.

The story spun out through *Forbes*, ESPN, all the ski magazines, and about thirty other media outlets. We suddenly saw ourselves under absurd headlines: "Youngest Owners of Ski Resort in the World Purchase Powder Mountain."

Word immediately spread, and all of our heroes lit up our phones.

"You guys did it? You actually pulled it off?"

"Congrats! What an accomplishment."

As the praise rolled in, we began to feel more and more uncomfortable. We had been so focused on a strategy to raise the final money that we had glossed over the fact that we hadn't actually accomplished our goal yet. We quickly called everyone who had reached out to us to let them know that we hadn't in fact closed, but we were getting very close.

We still needed to get $10 million more into the escrow account, but we figured that with all the interest now pouring in, we might need only one more extension from the owner before we could finally close.

We knew the press alone wasn't a guarantee that we'd attract our final investors. We needed to make one last bold move. Something to say that Summit was here to stay. We decided it was time to execute on an idea we'd been planning for a while: the SkyLodge.

For months we'd watched as the 144-square-foot hut we'd hastily constructed on a set of skis became a focal point for our guests. It was where we'd all congregate at sunset to swap stories of the day. We had dreamed of expanding on this concept and building a spacious lodge for our guests to connect over meals and après-ski.

We connected with a forward-thinking architect out of Portland who pitched us on a prefabrication concept. It sounded amazing: You design the lodge with the firm, they build the structure offsite, then they deliver it to you on eighteen-wheelers for a thirty-six-hour installation. The way they put it, prefabrication sort of sounded like buying a new car: You pay for it, they build it, give you the keys, and it's yours to drive off.

We felt confident we could erect a six-thousand-square-foot modern-day yurt on top of the mountain in no time. We went to the owners and pitched them on the concept, and they agreed to let us construct the lodge, with one caveat: If we weren't able to close on the mountain, the owners got to keep the building. It made sense, since we were essentially building a structure on land we didn't yet own. It was a multimillion-dollar bet, but we felt this structure would be the tipping point in bringing our vision into reality.

We quickly got to work on the design process. We were trying to create a new type of architecture in our development—we called it "heritage modernism." The idea behind the Sky-Lodge was to reimagine the classic yurt and bring it to life with heritage materials like barn wood in combination with a more modern aesthetic. It had 360-degree floor-to-ceiling windows, recessed seating, and a wrap-around deck complete with fire pits and an external ski locker room. In all our research, we hadn't seen anything like it, and we couldn't wait for it to come to life. We expedited the design process and moved right into production. Over the course of several months the entire lodge was constructed in a warehouse in the Pacific Northwest, broken down into shippable parts, and loaded onto semi-trailers that slowly inched their way to Eden. We burst with excitement when we saw the trucks roll in on a Monday afternoon. We figured by Friday we'd have the entire structure built and we'd be ready to wow our weekend guests in the new space.

But our enthusiasm quickly faded when we realized the mess we found ourselves in. First, we learned we had to dig the foundation for the SkyLodge and pour the concrete within an eighth of an inch of the specs on the blueprints, or the prefabricated structures wouldn't fit. Then, when we unloaded the truck and laid everything out, it looked like a disaster zone. Mirrors, tiles, and toilets had broken apart in transport. Two yurts came unassembled like a box of Legos. It was a complete mess, and it took our team *a month* to complete the assembly, not a day and a half. With all the modifications required and the additional cost of the concrete foundation, the whole project exceeded the original budget by 200 percent.

And yet it was even more beautiful and effective than we'd imagined.

The building was constructed at an altitude of nine thousand feet on a spot with the best views on the entire mountain. When you walked inside and took in the view, it felt like you were peering out over the edge of the world. You were so high up that you could see over the next set of mountains into the Great Salt Lake, which looked like an ocean.

The yurt was filled with ornate rugs, pillows, and furry blankets everywhere, and at the heart of the yurt was an open kitchen where everyone could congregate. It was stocked with bone broth, warming soups, and vegan and gluten-free treats. The snack bar was like our own version of the Sugar Shack, but this time we were actually invited to be there.

As beautiful as the SkyLodge was, the delays in construction only added to the pressure we felt as our timeline to close on the mountain got shorter and shorter. But with the momentum from the press and the SkyLodge now open, we were convinced that with just a little more time we'd be able to raise the money to close the deal. On April 15, filled with exuberance, we called up the owner. But their response to our eighth request for an extension was unlike any of the first seven.

"Congrats on the press, guys," the person overseeing the sale said. "But you all have a problem."

He told us that when we'd announced we were going to buy the mountain, we'd attracted a lot of attention. Now they had another offer that was the same as ours. In fact, the people behind it were planning to take a helicopter tour tomorrow.

"We're not going to renegotiate again. You can either close on April 24 at 5 P.M., as stipulated in our latest agreement, or we're going to take the other offer."

Our stomachs tightened.

We can't lose this now. We're too close.

Things quickly went from bad to worse when one of our biggest supporters decided to back out. He emailed the law firm seeking the return of his deposit on a $2 million homesite. When we called his team in desperation, they wouldn't explain why. After a while, they stopped returning our calls. *Why?* we wondered. We were counting on that money.

But there was no time to mourn the loss of that crucial cash. We needed to focus on how we were going to replace it with new prospects, and how we were going to dig out of the hole we were in, a hole that seemed to be getting deeper by the day.

The four of us convened in the SkyLodge, looking around at what we had just created. We were about to lose it all if we didn't immediately secure the funds to close.

"They're bluffing, right?"

"Tough to tell. But what choice do we have other than to call them on it?"

The current owners drove a tough bargain, and by this point in the negotiation, we were accustomed to them throwing elbows in order to optimize their position. We went to sleep confident that we could renegotiate and secure one last extension.

We woke up with a sense of renewed hope. The four of us

strategized over breakfast at the SkyLodge about our angle on the eighth extension, and what we thought was a realistic new closing date that they might agree to.

We had taken a break to walk out onto the deck overlooking the valley below when we heard the elegant rumble of an A-Star helicopter approaching. We all stood outside speechless, staring at the sleek helicopter circling in the air above us.

"Oh, my God."

"They're gonna take our mountain!"

The time for extensions was over. We either needed to close the deal or risk losing our home, and our reputations, forever.

37

THE ROAD TO SUCCESS IS ALWAYS UNDER CONSTRUCTION

We'll never know if it was just a random helicopter or if the passengers were from a development company that could've written a check for $40 million as easily as signing a credit card receipt after lunch.

It really didn't matter. We were out of time. We had to make the deadline.

And frankly, as long as we thought we could keep getting extensions, we didn't need to fully commit—and neither did our community. But as soon as we began to tell people, "April 24 is the day that we have to wire in the money or we don't get the mountain," our community started rallying in an entirely different way.

We had to become decisive in ways we hadn't been before. We had looked at bringing in outside lenders in case we couldn't secure all the financing ourselves. There were opportunities to raise money with a traditional resort developer, but they would've owned half the project. Not to mention that their money would've come from investors looking for a multiple on their return, which would've put us on shaky ground. *We'll give you the $40 million you need, but we're going to need to get $100 million back. That means we're going to need to build three times as many houses, and we're going to need to charge twice as much for lift tickets.* We knew that wouldn't please the Summit community *or* the town of Eden.

We put our foot down and refused to take that money because, for us, the most important thing was not the return on investment but the return on community. And when we say community, that didn't mean the few homebuyers. We meant for *everybody* who was throwing their heart into what we were creating, as well as the Eden locals. For every maker who didn't feel that there was a physical destination that embodied the values of entrepreneurship, collaboration, and open-mindedness.

We had a deep belief—maybe even a delusional one—that we were going to close. Sometimes you can feel like everything is just going to work out, but the truth is, that's blind optimism. And optimism alone can't wire you $20 million.

We only had seven days to make this happen. We barricaded ourselves in a ten-by-ten-foot room at the lake house. We called it the "peace room" instead of the "war room," because we weren't at war—we were bringing people together. There was one wooden table in the center, and whiteboards to track our progress stretched across three of the walls. Few people entered, and if anybody had wandered by, they might've thought they were passing a twenty-four-hour call center.

Each of us had a long list of names written out on legal pads in front of us: potential investors who were on the fence, guests who had spent a weekend and had shown interest, friends who had simply mentioned the words "mountain," "skiing," and "home" in the same sentence. The four of us ferociously dialed our phones, desperately trying to convince the voice on the other end that now was the time to commit.

We felt like we were back in Boca Raton wrangling forty entrepreneurs to the White House. At least now our leads were warmer and we didn't have to share beds.

But there will be no attempt here to create a heroic scene of us making dramatic calls and smoothly closing million-dollar investments one by one until we reached our $20 million down payment at 4:59 P.M.

No. It was much messier.

When we'd call people to get documents signed, they'd tell us they'd be happy to. *In fact,* they'd say, *let's get this done because I'm turning off my phone and going on a family trip next week.*

The documents would arrive as promised—but then someone in our office would gasp: *I can't believe this. They missed the signature on page thirty-seven!*

Many people didn't seem to understand our sense of urgency. *Whatever you need, I'd love to help you,* we'd read in an email. *Consider me your biggest supporter. Copying my assistant, and I can be available anytime next week.*

No, no, no! we felt like saying. *We need it this week, otherwise we're not going to be able to buy the mountain!*

We felt like we were air traffic controllers who had to land five 747s within a few minutes of each other on a single runway. *Land the entitlements. Next! Land the letter of intent on the county bond. Next! Land the private placement memorandums. Next!*

In the end, we didn't come in at $20 million. We went

from $10 million to well over *$20 million* in the escrow account in less than seven days. It was a true testament to the power of the community and the trust they were willing to put in us.

It happened so quickly that we were shell-shocked. We had that feeling you get when you sprint on a treadmill for a long time and then step off. Your body still feels like it's propelling itself forward even though you've slowed down. As elated as we were that we had just secured $30 million, we still had knots in our stomachs. By this point in our journey, we'd learned that nothing was guaranteed. Until those signatures were scribbled on the dotted line, none of us would rest easy.

At noon on April 24, 2013, Elliott drove to Salt Lake City to our law firm's office, where he met Greg and stepped into the largest conference room he had ever seen. The table had space for twenty-five seats on each side, but there were no chairs. Instead, the area for every seat was occupied by a huge stack of papers several inches thick.

Once all those contracts were signed, the four of us would own the mountain and have Greg as our partner. Elliott started signing for us, and his hands kept moving as blisters started to form between his fingers. He stopped only to massage away the cramps that kept returning, then continued until every document was complete.

Afterward, Greg left and Elliott hopped in his car and headed to the lake house to meet up with the three of us. Then something extraordinary happened: nothing. At the conclusion of nearly every one of our triumphs over the years, we'd gone somewhere to celebrate—sometimes even heading to the airport after an event and unwinding with a trip to a sun-soaked locale in a foreign country. On this night, however, there was none of that. We felt we were already in the most spectacular setting we could imagine, but there was no party to be had. We sprawled across four couches in the lake house and stared at the ceiling, basking in the exhilaration of what we'd accomplished, too exhausted to even speak. After a long silence, we sat up and simply smiled at each other.

Looking back, we can see it was a defining moment. Buying a mountain was an entirely different experience for the four of us than throwing events. With an event, we could be behind the eight-ball leading up to it, but with enough effort and sleepless nights, we'd come through at the last moment to save it. And once it was finished, it didn't matter that we'd been so frantic only a few days before. It was now over, and we were already firing off ideas about the possibilities for our next one. Developing a village on a mountain was an entirely different beast. There is no buzzer that announces you've won and sends everyone home with a prize. The game just keeps on rolling. We may have felt like we'd just crossed a finish line of sorts, but we were wary of what lay ahead.

All we'd really accomplished was breaking a sweat during warm-ups and getting ourselves into a game that we didn't fully understand—even with all of our earnestness and best intentions.

The four of us now looked at one another, older and much wiser, knowing that whatever challenges lay ahead of us, we would fight through them together.

You see, every business is going to face tremendous obstacles—maybe it's raising capital or maybe it's even a Great Recession. And you're going to have to fight, with everything you have, to get through them. To come out stronger on the other side.

If you've made small plans, what will you do when the obstacles become monumental? It's too easy to walk away from something small that doesn't really mean that much to you.

But if your plans are so audacious, so outlandish and big, that if you succeed you will change the lives of your family, your community, and perhaps even the world—well, then you will fight down to the marrow in your bones to keep all that you've created alive. Not only for yourself but for the world at large. Because, as we've said, the world needs these kinds of plans—now more than ever.

And so, it's through all of our challenges, stumbles, and victories that we've learned our most important lesson, one worthy of the title of this book—and of the big dream you're about to pursue.

Make no small plans.

As an entrepreneur, you face a financial dilemma the day you decide to start your company; you're forced to navigate the balancing act between capital and responsibility. If you bootstrap your start-up and you fail, the only person you let down is yourself. But if you raise money for your company, well, now you're selling your dream to somebody else, and convincing *them* to believe in *you*. When you take on an investor, you become responsible for their money, and if you fail, you're not just letting yourself down, you're disappointing the people who believed in you.

We'd always bootstrapped Summit, ever since our first event in Park City. We had put our initial expenses on credit cards and scrambled to bring in sponsorship dollars until eventually we were able to establish a revenue model relying primarily on ticket sales.

When we first discovered Powder Mountain in 2011, we knew that for the first time in our company's history, we'd need to turn to outside investors. We spent the subsequent years selling our dream to a group of people who shared our vision for a utopian village on top of a mountain—a place to host our celebrations and raise our kids. Eventually, forty founding members believed in the vision of Powder Mountain and invested in our dream. So we had to make sure we delivered on that promise.

We believed we had all of our bases covered. We had a business partner who had found the mountain and who was responsible for the finance and all the things we weren't well suited for at that time. We brought our community and connections, hospitality partners, and were responsible for designing the master plan and architectural vernacular.

Unfortunately, we had severely underestimated what it would take to bring our vision to life. Up until this point, all of our knowledge and experience had been gained through short sprints toward multi-day gatherings. In three days of fireworks, with so much energy and action at every turn, attendees would spin through the event on a whirlwind adventure, with no time for them—or us—to recognize any of our blind spots. Even if small failures occurred, we'd chalk them up as a learning experience and vow to do better next time.

With the mountain, there was no "next time." We had always known we had only one shot. And our shot was dependent on other people beyond our four-person founding brotherhood. Nearly a decade of event production experience could never have prepared us for the depth of complexity involved in master-planning an entire town at an elevation of eight thousand feet. We were dumbfounded by how long, arduous, and nonlinear a process it was to develop land.

From Summit's inception, we had always set wildly ambitious goals. But through perseverance, creativity, and some luck, we had always been able to pull things off. Yet despite all the feats we had overcome in the past, the development of

Powder Mountain was by far the most humbling experience we had ever faced.

With the development, it felt as though we were pushing a boulder up our mountain for years. There were many points in our journey when we wanted to stop, rest, or just coast for a while. But we knew that we had to resist this instinct. We knew that if we did, the boulder would roll back down the hill, getting heavier and harder to push each time around whenever we decided to get back to work. We also knew that there'd be plenty of time to rest when we got to the other side. We learned that the key was to keep moving forward, despite the odds, despite the frustrations.

All the challenges we faced with the mountain became our greatest teachers. They taught us how to communicate more, how to be *better*. Better entrepreneurs. Better communicators. Better partners.

As the age-old adage goes: "You never fail until you stop trying."

In the early days of Summit, to help push ourselves past our comfort zones, we'd rattle off a punchy one-liner to each other: "If you're not scared, it won't make the movie." It was our way of pressuring each other to lean into discomfort and go big. We'd imagined a director making a movie about our life at that moment, and would ask ourselves, *Would this scene be interesting? Would there be a sense of danger or risk that would captivate an audience? Or would our character get cut from the film?*

We found this exercise to be both fun and effective. It motivated us to take more chances and push the boundaries of what we thought was possible with our business.

As much as this exercise helped us in our formative years, as the four of us and our company matured, we discovered that the behind-the-scenes mundane work was just as important to the success of a company as the high-risk high-reward behavior. It just might not make the film's final cut.

The same concept can be seen in movies about the building of companies. They generally focus on the wild ups and downs of the early years—and there is a good reason for this framing. The craziness at the beginning of a business makes for the best stories, even though the maturity and massive growth of the company typically occur afterward. The advances that arise as a company scales generally come through decisions made in everyday meetings that are a part of a business's daily life. All of which is crucial—but which outsiders might see as boring.

It's why *The Social Network* only focuses on the inception and first few years of Facebook. Or why *The Founder* showcases Ray Kroc's cunning mind as he worked to take over and expand McDonald's in its early days.

Our story is no different. For years we had continually pushed all of our chips into the middle of the table, believing in ourselves enough to be willing to risk everything time and time again. But as we grew, we reached a point where we needed to slow down, be more methodical, and pace ourselves. We needed to be more strategic with our time and energy, and mitigate risk while charting a path forward.

Though this period at Summit wouldn't get much play in a movie, it was filled with bursts of improvements at our events and a slow transformation of the mountain. This was a time where we put our lessons to good use, trusted experts, admitted our weaknesses, corrected our course, and tuned our compass.

We learned that circumstances change as a business evolves. We were more open to trusting people who had done it all before. We wanted to learn from and work with people who loved to lead: executives who empowered our teams to find their purpose and be inspired each day.

The right partners can make your business run more smoothly and efficiently. They may take pressure off. That said, the less conflict your business bumps up against, the less it's going to interest the movie director.

That is why you won't see a chapter in this book about cutting a road through our mountain, even though it's a highly specialized operation whose importance can't be overlooked. The process is filled with a great deal of tension because it costs millions of dollars and it has to be done precisely. You don't get a second chance at laying a road on the edge of a cliff. And while a few people might be intrigued by every detail of the process, most will rather just drive on the road than get bogged down in the minutiae of what it takes to build it.

We were now in our thirties and no longer hanging off trains, nor were we eating, sleeping, and breathing the same air together twenty-four hours a day. Jeff and Elliott both got married a month apart in 2016 at Powder Mountain, and Jeremy would meet his future wife around that time as well. All three met their significant others through the Summit community. Jeff and Elliott caught up on a little sleep before they both became fathers within two years of each other and the sleepless nights began again. Brett planted deeper roots in Eden, purchasing a home and inviting his parents to move in four doors down so that he could spend more quality time with them.

We remained true to our vision to keep the small-town

charm that made Powder Mountain a feel-good throwback, and many neighbors in the valley began to take notice and join in our vision. They showed up to talk about it at our weekly "Pizza and Pints" dinners. They reached out to say thanks for the thirty miles of public mountain biking trails that we'd built.

They realized that the ski experience had become better than it ever had been, in part because we made sure limits were placed on season passes as well as a cap on the number of lift tickets that could be sold every day. There were no crowds, no parking problems, and nobody ever had to wait for a lift. Yet at the same time, the team we'd assembled brought in ever-increasing amounts of revenue at the resort.

We didn't move as swiftly in the development of Powder Mountain as we would've liked, and we're the first to admit that we promised too much and trusted others' promises to us too innocently. And while there was disappointment over our pace, we knew that with time we'd do everything in our power to deliver on our word.

We could remember a time out of college when we viewed LinkedIn as a place to look for a job, and now we were hosting the company's founder, Reid Hoffman, at Summit. We could recall dissecting Eckhart Tolle's books when we'd first arrived in Nicaragua, and now we had him onstage at our event in downtown Los Angeles. We'd invested early in Uber through connections made at Summit, and now Uber's new CEO was being interviewed at one of our gatherings. We had once not known what to do with dozens of boxes of leftover tequila packed into our South Beach hotel room, and now we had a program that allowed us to recycle used wine bottles and turn them into glasses, as well as build event spaces using previous events' waste products and boxes.

In the early days many attendees had asked why there weren't more women present, and now more than 50 percent of our attendees—and our team—were female. We stopped to marvel at the mini Central Park our team had brought to life in thirty-six hours over a thirty-thousand-square-foot parking area for our event in downtown Los Angeles. Twelve thousand meals were served every day at the event, and it stood up to any food festival on the planet, while fifty thousand meals were extended to the unhoused.

We had evolved to a level where we could make a difference in the lives of people who never even bought a ticket to one of our events. We created a fellowship program, which gave scholarships to young entrepreneurs and paired them with founders and funders to make changes in the multiplicity of areas and issues we wanted to see improved in the world. We helped launch a Criminal Justice Policy Lab that looked at the terrible treatment of inmates, brought Summit attendees into the prisons to meet inmates, hosted talks, and put together policy for incarceration reform.

After overcoming countless trials and obstacles, we had reached a gratifying place by the beginning of 2020. We'd hosted the most sophisticated annual flagship event in our history, brought in our highest revenues, created a platform to facilitate our largest donations to date, and devised our most innovative business plan to scale Summit exponentially.

Forbes had once referred to Summit as the "Davos of the next generation," and though we'd always been careful about such superlatives, we started to think that perhaps we'd finally begun to earn that moniker.

And then, suddenly, we were flipped upside down along with the rest of the world.

When the pandemic hit, it felt like we were back to square one, fighting for our company's survival.

But we weren't going to give up that easily. When we looked back at the sum of the feats that we had managed to pull off—from chartering a commercial jet to befriending presidents and world leaders—we turned our beginners' mindsets back on. It felt like we were in start-up mode once again—except this time we had more than a decade of experiences to draw from and many mentors to call upon. Filled with excitement, we got to work brainstorming solutions. We knew that no matter what problem might arise, we were only an idea away.

ACKNOWLEDGMENTS

We would like to start off by thanking and acknowledging the entire Summit community. Through your support, you have given us the opportunity to pursue our dreams. We will never be able to thank you enough for all that you've done for us. Please know we are always at your service.

We want to thank all of our team members, collaborators, and partners across the Summit organization. Although this book tells stories of specific team members and their contributions, it should by no means diminish the importance of every past and present team member who has dedicated parts of their lives to helping fulfill the vision of Summit. We are forever indebted to you.

Thank you to everyone who has helped in the making of this book; we are so grateful to have worked with such amazing and talented people: Cal Fussman for your Herculean efforts in distilling our story into written form, Ryan Holiday for all of your hard work in distilling many of our stories into tangible lessons and real-life takeaways. Our wonderful editors Georgia Francis King, Kevin Mcdonnell, and Sarah Panzer. Alex Banayan for your guidance from concept to completion. Our agent Byrd Leavell. Roger Scholl for taking a chance on us. Matt Inman for your invaluable feedback and guidance throughout the whole process. And special thanks to Ray Dalio, who implored us to write this book, explained to us that our actions were in fact reflective of our principles, and that those principles have value.

Thank you to everyone who took the time to read the early versions of our manuscript and provide valuable feedback to us. You've helped make this book so much better than we thought possible.

Thank you to the Summit Powder Mountain team, who has literally moved mountains with us: The level of executive guidance and the incredible body of work that took us from acquisition to building neighborhoods is beyond comparison, and we're deeply indebted to you for making it happen.

Thank you to Langely McNeal and Jess Berne Strombelline for all of your help along our journey.

We are eternally grateful for the incredible families who've joined our Powder Mountain journey as neighbors and collaborators. In particular, the Founding Members who leapt off the cliff with us, and enabled us to purchase the mountain in the first place, and the neighbors who have served in board and directorial capacities over the years. Without you, the project would not have happened. We truly can't thank you enough.

Deep gratitude is due to the funding partners of the Summit Impact Foundation, The Summit Fellowship, and the Summit Institute. Thank you for your financial, moral, and intellectual support and guidance as we've strived to utilize our platform to maximize the good we can create in the world.

We are very appreciative of the Summit Impact Foundation board members: Heather Hartnett, Jessica Jackley, Christina Sass, Hank Willis Thomas, Ellen Gustafson, Greg Hoffman, Cristina Falcone, and Arlan Hamilton.

Thank you to the Summit Junto investors and board members as well as the Summit Series Lifetime members. You all stepped up when we needed you most, and have gone above and beyond to underwrite the Summit platform. Without you, we wouldn't be here.

We are blessed with an abundance of family and friendships that we owe the vast majority of our success to. And while this book is over, we would have to double the length of this print to properly cover the multitude of dear friends, mentors, collaborators, and supporters to whom we owe a debt of gratitude—you know who you are. We stand on the shoulders of giants, and we'll never forget it. Thank you.

ELLIOTT BISNOW WOULD LIKE TO PERSONALLY THANK:
My grandmother, Florence; my parents, Mark and Margot; my brother, Austin; and my wife, Nicole. I'd also like to thank Vesa Ponkka, Martin Blackman, and Jarred Snyder for your belief in me for so many years. And, to my son, Lumi, I hope you enjoy reading your dad's story. :)

JEFF ROSENTHAL WOULD LIKE TO PERSONALLY THANK:
My wife, Julia; my children, River and Siena; my parents, Jim and Lisa; and my sisters, Nancy Pink and Grace San Soucie.

BRETT LEVE WOULD LIKE TO PERSONALLY THANK:
My parents, Michael and Betsy; my brother, Erik; and my sister, Brooke Baker. I'd also like to thank Jay Baitler and Mark Anstine for all your help along the way.

JEREMY SCHWARTZ WOULD LIKE TO PERSONALLY THANK:

My wife, Abby; my parents, Joel and Casey; my brother, Kevin; and my sister, Jaime. Thank you for your love, support, and guidance all of these years. You have truly helped shape me into the person I am today.

INDEX

ABOUT THE AUTHORS

ELLIOTT BISNOW, BRETT LEVE, JEFF ROSENTHAL, and JEREMY SCHWARTZ are the founders of Summit, a portfolio of companies that includes Summit Series, a global events company best known for creating immersive events and experiences for a community of entrepreneurs from around the world. They are the co-owners of the largest ski resort in the United States, Powder Mountain; co-manage Summit's consumer tech venture fund, the Summit Action Fund; and are actively involved with Conservation International, Beyond Conflict, the Council on Foreign Relations, the Anti-Recidivism Coalition, and the Drawdown Fund. All four founders are sought-after speakers and have been featured in *The New York Times, The Wall Street Journal, The Economist, Bloomberg Businessweek, Time,* and *Fast Company.*

www.summit.co